The Short Stories of Larry Potterfield - Volume 1

ISBN 978-0-578-16261-4

The Short Stories of
Larry Potterfield

Volume 1

~ Introduction ~

Dad taught me to hunt and fish, back when I was growing up on the farm in northeast Missouri. Things were much simpler in the '50s and I can't imagine what my life would be like today, had I not enjoyed the benefit of all the instruction of those early years. I shot my first duck at age 9 and my first quail at 13 - the same year I got my first gun for Christmas - a hand-me-down Stevens 16 gauge single shot.

Some of my fondest memories are the hunting and fishing stories Dad and my uncles shared with us kids back then - generally around the wood stove, and other times in the field. Unfortunately, it was pure and simple storytelling, so all I have are the memories. Now, as a father and grandfather and having hunted and fished all my life, I am taking the time to write down some of my own stories – for the enjoyment of my children, grandchildren, friends and Customers.

Only a handful of the images in this book were taken by professional photographers, the rest were taken by family, professional hunters, guides and myself, with whatever camera technology we had at the time. When it comes to quality images, you will see continuous improvement on the later stories, versus the earlier ones.

The very nature of a Short Story doesn't provide an opportunity to mention all of the people who were there; my apologies to family, friends, professional hunters, guides, trackers and other staff, who were in the background or foreground of these stories, but aren't mentioned. For most of these stories, other people were also there and possibly saw or remember things differently; my apologies for any inaccuracies or omissions. These are all real stories that I participated in, nothing is made up; and I write them purely for your enjoyment.

~ Dedication ~

A man who writes a dedication, without putting his family first, has a big hole in his life that will never fill up. My parents, brothers and sister, wife and children – and even grandchildren, have all played a critical role in shaping my life, my experiences and my way of thinking. Many are also subjects of these stories.

Dad deserves a lot of credit, because he taught me to hunt and fish, to hunt for mushrooms, to tend the honey bees and all things hunting and fishing – and on the farm. Mom encouraged the education, homework and chores around the house. Both are gone now, but forever in my memories.

Brother Jerry was keenly important in getting MidwayUSA started, back in 1977, and was a full partner in the business for the first three years. This book wouldn't be possible without the success of Midway and getting off to the right start was critical. And of course, without the NRA, Safari Club International and the other Key Conservation Groups, there wouldn't be many guns or much hunting or fishing.

Brenda and I have been married for 45 years and have two children and six grandchildren. She took up hunting about 20 years back and you will see her in many of these stories. In my mind, it isn't possible to overestimate the importance of a supportive wife, and children and grandchildren - with manners and values that you can be proud of.

The Employees of MidwayUSA, most especially the Senior Leadership Team and Middle Leadership Team, have been tremendously supportive of this work and have done a great job of running the business – allowing me the time off to hunt and fish and write these stories.

Lastly, I don't want to forget the outfitters, guides, professional hunters, trackers and staff who worked such long hours every day to ensure that we hunters and fishermen enjoyed the very best that nature had to offer.

Larry Potterfield

MidwayUSA | Columbia, Missouri | 13 April 2015

~ Table of Contents ~

~ Table of Contents ~

DANGEROUS GAME
of *Africa*

The origin of the term 'Dangerous Game' is likely lost in the ancient folklore of Africa. Roosevelt used the term in his book *African Game Trails*, detailing his safari of 1909/10, and the five animals he identified as such are the same ones we talk about today.

Lion, leopard, Cape buffalo, elephant and rhinoceros are considered to be the dangerous game of Africa; everything else is thought of as 'Plains Game'. Both the hippopotamus and the crocodile can be dangerous to the natives, but not enough so to professional hunters or clients as to make the list.

In my mind, elephant are the most dangerous; if you get too close, they are going to come for you. Rhino are the same – but to a lesser extent, and there aren't so many of them today. Typically lion, leopard and buffalo are not problematic until you get a poorly placed bullet into them, at which time the buffalo is the most dangerous of the three — because it takes a direct hit to the brain or spine to stop him.

An elephant that is shot in the brain often simply collapses, as this one did – while running at full speed. Notice the typical cracks in the pads of the feet; like fingerprints, no two are the same. Also, please notice the small tuft of thick hair on the tip of the tail.

The LAST TEN SECONDS
of an Elephant Hunt

It had been a long and impossible track, interrupted by the wind, the rain and a group of females; but we had seen him for a few seconds, just 20 minutes into the track, and knew this was a bull we couldn't give up on.

Twice during the morning we had lost his track; then, quite by accident, we found it again – and shortly we were on him.

There were seven of us on the track, three trackers in the front, then the professional hunter (PH), myself, Brenda and finally the game scout. We were walking slowly but deliberately through light brush, on dry grass and leaves – about two or three steps apart.

Unknown to any of us, the bull had turned sharply off his line a few yards in front of us, walked slightly up hill and was standing in sight and sound of our small group.

We were making way too much noise when the number three tracker spotted him. Now begins the last ten seconds of our elephant hunt.

All three trackers hurriedly collapsed back down the line, as the PH and I moved forward to the front; the second tracker handed off my rifle as he went by – four seconds.

My first responsibility, as the hunter, was to check the scope levers, the scope power and the safety – two seconds; then I looked for the bull, knowing only that he was to our left.

There he was, broadside at 40 yards, slightly uphill through the brush, head up, and very nervous. The PH said "shoot him now!"

The white portion of the tusk was in the skull, stopping near the eye.

Unknown at the moment, we later discovered that the bullet had shot through this six inch tree, on the way to the elephant.

The tusks weigh 55 and 56 pounds and are just under 6 feet in length.

On elephant there is often a choice between a brain shot and a heart shot.

I took another step forward to clear some brush and brought my gun into position, thinking about bullet placement, the shoulder or the brain – two seconds. But, immediately he charged.

It was pure instinct; shoot for the brain – cross hairs between the eye and the ear, keep the barrel moving and pull the trigger. At 25 yards, the bull and the Hornady 375 solid met head on – two seconds. His front legs collapsed and he slid the full length of his body – game over.

So that was the last ten seconds of our elephant hunt.

Mkuyu Camp | Selous Game Reserve | Tanzania, Africa | 29 November 2011

The ELEPHANT I ALMOST Didn't Shoot

This picture was taken at about 40 yards, as we abandoned our first approach. The bull never knew we were there, and was simply flapping his ears to keep cool.

Judging the length and weight of elephant tusks is challenging, even for experienced professional hunters; and poor judgment could cost a PH his license.

Our routine was to leave camp each morning just after 6:00 a.m., when there was enough light to see fresh elephant tracks crossing the dirt roads. It was now the eighth day; we had tracked up a few bulls, but nothing interesting. After lunch, we eased the safari car quietly into a large clearing that held some water. Our PH had seen a crocodile there on an earlier safari and he wanted to take another look.

As we came into the clearing, there were two elephant bulls walking away at the far end, perhaps 800 yards. We stopped the car and looked briefly with our binoculars and then began a quick advance on foot. The rear bull had the biggest ivory I had seen, but what did I know?

We left the rest of the team in the shade about 150 yards out and the PH and I proceeded alone, to a small bush about 40 yards away. We looked him over carefully and it was obvious that my young PH was in a quandary. Was this a shooter or not? He finally decided no. I took a few pictures and we backed out.

The PH, speaking in Swahili, related the story to the others. There was quite a bit of discussion and the game scout was quite animated. Then, in English, the PH said that the game scout was insistent this bull was big enough to shoot and that he would take full responsibility, if the bull was under the legal minimum. "So, what did I want to do?"

Easy choice, I had thought he was a shooter at first sight. So, the PH and I made the short trip back to the bull, nearly in the position we left him. He was facing us and we walked straight in. At about 20 steps he noticed us, raised his head and started toward us. My first shot for the brain was a little high; as he turned to run, I put one between his eye and ear and he was down for the count. The elephant I almost didn't shoot had the longest tusks of anything I have shot since.

Luwele Camp | Selous Game Reserve | Tanzania, Africa | 19 August 2001

12

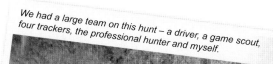
We had a large team on this hunt – a driver, a game scout, four trackers, the professional hunter and myself.

The trackers are Maasai and this is their traditional garb in camp and back home. My rifle is a Charles Boswell Double, in 500 3-1/4" Nitro Express.

We finished processing the elephant just at dark. Fresh elephant heart was our hors d'oeuvre before heading back to camp. PH Nicolas Negre.

During lunch break one day, PH Nicolas Negre and I strip and clean his Weatherby Mark V 460 Weatherby.

Brenda's MONSTER LEOPARD

Here's the traditional pose that Leopard hunters picture themselves in. This is a very big, old male leopard and Brenda could only hold it this way for a few seconds. Notice a tracker's hand holding the leopard's head up.

A ny male leopard is a great trophy; but sometimes, in far away and remote places, you find a real monster. We were hunting in Maasailand, in northern Tanzania, just below the border with Kenya. The principle vegetation there is thorn bush and grass. The area is sparsely populated by the Maasai and Dorobo tribes, who have lived there, with little change, for thousands of years. The Maasai herd sheep and cattle and the Dorobo, who curiously speak the same language, are hunter/gatherers.

There are a few dirt roads that the outfitter grades each year before the hunting season, but mostly there are just trails through the thorn bushes, created by the livestock. Our trackers were all Maasai and one day a young herdsman waived us down to say that he had seen the tracks of a huge leopard at a distant waterhole with no access by road.

Labor is pretty cheap there – one dollar per day per person, so our PH had one of our trackers and a team of four locals cut in a road to the waterhole. They used nothing but corn knives and it took four days; then we drove three hours to the waterhole, hung an impala leg for bait and drove out.

Brenda was the one that wanted a big leopard, but since my car knew how to get there, we checked the bait. It was nearly noon when we arrived and the leopard had fed the night before, but Brenda was in the other safari car, three or more hours away. We were able to get a message to her PH by radio and asked them to bring some 'overnight supplies', as we didn't want to drive the new road in the night. We built a blind, cleared a place for our camp a mile or so away and cut and piled a thorn bush barricade to keep out the wild critters.

The dining area of base camp; we missed it that night.

In some camps, it's a tradition to burn the leopard blind, after the hunt is over.

After the leopard is shot or an old bait is abandoned, one of the trackers climbs the tree and cuts the rope.

This was our spike camp – way out in the bush. The trackers piled thorn brush around the perimeter and took turns keeping the fire going all night long, watching for lions and hyenas.

Brenda Arrived at 4:30 p.m. and went directly to the blind. In remote areas, leopard often come in during daylight hours and indeed the leopard showed up an hour later. After all this work, it was a one hour hunt, for the biggest leopard we have ever seen. We slept on tarps on the hard ground and drove happily back to base camp the next morning, with this monster leopard.

Luwele Camp | Selous Game Reserve | Tanzania, Africa | 9 August 2002

CLOSE ENCOUNTER
with Lions

This is a young male, without a mane.

It was Russell who was after a lion and we had hung baits in many places but hadn't seen any lion tracks. Late in the safari, and a few days after the full moon, it was suggested that Russell and his PH might walk in on one of the baits after the moon came up and sit for a few hours, in case something came in. The other PH had a varmint call, and I suggested that they take it along and perhaps do some calling.

For this bait, they had set up a ground blind – a simple, three-sided affair facing the bait across the arm of a small lake. There were two chairs, but no back side to the blind. The trail that led to the blind had been swept clean of leaves and sticks, so they could walk in quietly and possibly sneak up on lions feeding. They snuck in ok, using the light of the full moon, but there was nothing there; so they sat down and waited.

The PH had nonchalantly leaned his rifle up against a tree behind the blind and positioned Russell's rifle on a rest pointing at the bait – and actually tied it in position.

After everything quieted down, the PH set up the varmint call and turned it on. Of course it made a horrific sound, designed specifically to call varmints. In retrospect, perhaps the speaker should have been positioned nearer the bait, than the hunters.

After a few minutes, for whatever reason, Russell looked back over his shoulder and saw three lions coming up the trail they had just walked a few minutes before – two females and a male. He poked the PH with his elbow and told him there were lions behind them and to shut off the call. The PH couldn't find the on/off switch, but was able to turn the volume to its lowest setting. The female that was in the front stopped two steps from the back of Russell's chair. Russell still shivers when he tells this story!

The lions stood there for a while, then laid down for a few minutes. When they got up, they circled the blind a couple of times, until they discovered the bait and went for it. Russell shot the male lion, which was a fitting end to the story.

Bill Bedford's Riverside Camp | Zimbabwe, Africa | 12 July 1997

Magnificent; that's the best way to describe the adult male lion. This one is probably 4-5 years old and of average size and mane.

Daughter Sara points at the closest track with her mom and the blind in the background.

In this part of Zimbabwe, giraffe are often used for lion bait.

Lion baits are hung low, so that a lion can just reach it while standing. Our PH points to a claw mark on the tree.

CAPE BUFFALO
with a Lever Action Rifle

Any mature buffalo bull is a trophy and over 40" in width is very special. This Winchester 1895 is 42" end to end.

My rifle was what Teddy Roosevelt referred to as "the medicine gun for lions" – a Winchester Model 1895 chambered in 405 Winchester. Teddy hunted Africa in 1909 and wrote up his adventures in *African Game Trails*. Now, I was in Africa, a century later, hunting Cape buffalo with a similar gun.

We cut the track of a single bull, near a dry creek bed, and off we went. There were two trackers, then the professional hunter (PH) and myself, followed by a third tracker (carrying water) and the game scout – six of us in total. We were walking quietly through open bush, going slightly downhill alongside the creek.

It was a quick stalk, barely ten minutes, when the PH spotted the bull bedded about a hundred and fifty yards out – good eyes!

The bull's head was just behind a tree that blocked his view of us. He was headed uphill, with his head to our left, and we could only see his left horn protruding from behind the tree. The PH and I proceeded on alone.

One quiet step after another we advanced, stopping behind a small bush about 40 yards from the bull.

Now, it was decision time – wait till he stands up, so we can see the other horn or take a chance and shoot him right there. We waited; but after only five minutes we got bored and decided to shoot.

Taking careful aim I fired. In one smooth motion, the bull came to his feet, turned 180 degrees and headed downhill. My thoughts came quickly: "He shouldn't have gotten up; this is a repeater; shoot him again." Levering in another round I put a second Woodleigh bullet into his shoulder – again, nothing happened. My third shot was high on the shoulder, hitting his spine, and he went down like a sack of potatoes. Three shots in about four seconds; the trackers were impressed with such firepower.

So that's my story of hunting Cape buffalo with a lever action rifle.

Luwele Camp | Selous Game Reserve | Tanzania, Africa | 8 December 2008

Brenda has shot several Cape buffalo, this one with son Russell's Winchester Model 70 in 416 Remington Mag.

Hunting is very traditional and, for me at least, a classic gun makes it even more so. My rifle on this hunt was a Winchester Model 1895, produced in 1904 and chambered in 405 Winchester. Daughter Sara, on the left.

Brenda and PH Nicolas Negre carry out a buffalo skull, from a kill deep in the brush.

President Theodore Roosevelt and buffalo skulls in Africa 1909. Also pictured are R.J. Cunninghame, Kermit Roosevelt, Edmund Heller and Hugh H. Heatley.

My
FIRST
CAPE
Buffalo

A Cape buffalo is one of the great trophies of Africa and you will never forget the first one.

Your first Cape buffalo will dance around in your mind for the rest of your life, not necessarily because of the size of the trophy, but rather because of the circumstances of the hunt - no matter how routine. We were driving by a large plain of tall grass; it holds a little water during the rainy season, but goes completely dry when the rains stop. Elephant and Cape buffalo love these places! Several hundred yards out into the grass we saw a lone bull, through an open area, and stopped to glass; but we never got a good look before he bedded down.

There was a small tree nearby, so one of the trackers and the PH scurried up to take a look. The PH never saw him; but the tracker, a bit higher in the tree, reported to the PH that this was a very big buffalo and that if we were to shoot him, it would be the biggest one to be shot in the camp the entire year. Well, that was a pretty good report, so off we went – the PH, one tracker and me, while the other tracker stayed in the tree to guide us to the buffalo we couldn't see.

We knew the shooting would be close, but I was well-armed with a double rifle in 500 Nitro Express. Son Russell says it's "a gun that's big enough to stop fights."

The ground was hard, dry and horribly rough, from the elephant and buffalo tracks; and the visibility was only a few yards. Every little bit we would look back at the tracker and he would motion left, right, or straight ahead, to keep us on course. The last few yards were painfully slow, and I began to get wired!

At nine steps, the bull stood up broadside, and we saw him for the first time. A buffalo, when surprised, will normally hesitate for a couple of seconds, trying to figure out what's going on, before he runs or charges; I was really wired by now and got a bullet high in his shoulder and through his spine in a few tenths of the first second.

Unfortunately, the high expectations for the trophy didn't match up with what lay on the ground, so the moral of this story is to never let a tracker judge the size of the trophy.

Luwele Camp | Selous Game Reserve | Tanzania, Africa | 14 July 1998

This is an old bull, with his horns well worn - clearly a trophy, though not in the traditional sense. Rifle is a Charles Boswell, made about 1912.

I learned to climb trees at an early age and enjoyed climbing them in Africa, in search of game.

When slightly spooked, buffalo will often pause for a few seconds to understand the problem. These six bulls were bedded at mid-day and we got to within 40 yards – no shooters.

This is just a 'fun' picture; the buffalo was quite dead before I laid down in front of him; no blood, no torn clothes, no missing parts.

The MEDICINE GUN for Lions

Upon returning to camp, the staff celebrated the success of the hunter, in killing the lion.

It's fair to call me traditional, plus I'm a gun collector and like to hunt. Rolling those three things together is the basis for this story. As a gun collector, old Winchester lever action rifles have always fascinated me. Everyone knows that the Winchester 1873 was the gun that won the west, but not as many people know about the last and most-powerful of these guns, the Model 1895. This model is best remembered for its most-powerful chambering, the 405 Winchester, and Teddy Roosevelt's referral to it as "the medicine gun for lions" in his famous African safari of 1909/1910. Most serious Winchester collections include a Winchester 1895 in 405 Winchester; mine certainly does.

But remember, I am not just a gun collector but also a hunter – a safari hunter; so it seemed perfectly logical for a traditional person like me to take my 405 to Africa and shoot a lion with it.

It was Brenda's safari car that first spotted the lion, guarding what was left of a buffalo he had killed the day before. Circling vultures had led them to the kill site. Fortunately for me, Brenda didn't have a lion license; so that evening over dinner my PH and I made plans to go after that lion first thing the next morning. Since the Model 1895 wasn't designed for a scope, it was important not to arrive before there was enough light to see the open sights.

The lion was two hours from camp, so we were up quite early, to arrive at first shooting light – 6:00 a.m.

We went in from downwind, very, very quietly through the bush and into the opening of the kill site, but the lion wasn't there – at least not where we thought he would be. But then he challenged us from a slightly different position, trotting straight toward his kill, and us, stopping about 125 yards out. It was a standoff for a few seconds; that was the limit of my range, but I wouldn't take a frontal shot. Then he turned and walked away, at which time my PH roared like a lion. The brute stopped and turned broadside.

My shot was on the mark and the 405 did its job, just as it had for Roosevelt a hundred years earlier.

Luwele Camp | Selous Game Reserve | Tanzania, Africa | 8 December 2003

A fine lion, shot with a grand old rifle.

Spotted hyena; the lion and hyena are mortal enemies.

My Winchester Model 1895 in 405 Winchester, serial # 47346 – made in 1904. Magazine holds four rounds of 405 ammo.

Group picture – from left, daughter Sara, Bob Zara, myself, PH Fred Blochet, Brenda and PH Eric Pasanis.

FRESH
ELEPHANT
HEART
For Lunch

It was a short track, mid-morning, on the third day of the safari. We were walking at a pretty good clip and came into an opening in the bush to discover the elephant standing about fifty yards to our right; facing us, but apparently asleep. One shot in the brain with the 375 H&H and the bull fell where he stood – never knowing we were on his track. We took lots of pictures and then began the long process of removing the tusks.

That's when I said to the PH: "Let's have fresh elephant heart for lunch." He had never done it before, but was game to give it a try.

Frederick Selous, and other ivory hunters of the 19th century, wrote about eating elephant heart. Every hunter had to feed his crew and with several tons of elephant meat on the ground, there wasn't any reason to waste ammunition or time shooting something else – meat is meat. Roosevelt hunted in 1909/1910 and wrote about eating elephant heart. So, I was just carrying on a tradition.

Now, removing the heart from an elephant is just like doing the same on an elk or a deer; well not exactly, you don't eviscerate an elephant. The first step is to slice away a three foot square of skin over the area of the heart; next, the ribs have to be cut with an axe to get into the body cavity. Actually removing the heart is now pretty straightforward, except that it's as big as a five gallon bucket.

I have eaten fresh moose meat and sheep meat at the kill site, up in the high meadows and on the mountainside, and can say that

Elephant tusks are often different lengths. The tusks grow continuously, but the thinner front end gets the wear and tear and regularly breaks off. The white portion is in the skull and is mostly hollow.

He was standing in an open area and this is just as he fell.
The PH took this picture from the top of the safari car.

Frederick Selous and Teddy Roosevelt wrote of cooking elephant heart at the kill site; so I was just carrying on the tradition. If prepared rare or medium rare, it is quite tender.

When I tell this story, typically someone wants to know how big an elephant heart is; now, you know. The tracker, Tangana, chopped the ribs with an axe, then cut out the heart with his knife. He is holding it upside down.

preparation is about the same, and it must be simple. First, I build a small fire; then cut some sticks that are long enough for cooking, without burning my hands. The meat is cut into small cubes that will cook quickly. If I'm fortunate enough to have salt and pepper, all the better; but it's certainly not necessary.

Of all my experiences in hunting, fresh elephant heart at the kill site ranks pretty high up on the list – for taste, as well as tradition – and to celebrate the success of the hunt.

Kibaoni Camp | Selous Game Reserve | Tanzania, Africa | 27 November 2009

Brenda displays the tusks, 47 and 53 pounds; no wonder she is smiling. The longer one is just over 6 feet around the outside curve.

SHOOT or NO-SHOOT,
an Unusual Elephant Hunt

Professional hunters tell me that judging the length and weight of the ivory on an elephant is just an educated guess, because it is so difficult to estimate the length of the tusks inside the skull and it is impossible to know the size of the root in the base of the tusks. Wildlife departments, professional hunters and clients usually have minimum requirements; so, there is always the question "shoot or no-shoot?"

I saw this elephant on the first day of our safari, in the middle of the afternoon. We had walked to a secluded water hole and found him drinking there all by himself. He looked like a shooter to me, but what do I know? My PH said he wasn't big enough, so I took some pictures and we left him. On day four Brenda and her PH, who had guided over a hundred elephant hunts, were at the same water hole, about the same time of day – and there he was again; but her PH also said he wasn't a shooter.

Around the dinner table at night we had plenty of conversation about this elephant. As it happened, Brenda's PH was only there for the first seven days, after which another PH was coming in. I jokingly made the comment that when the other PH came, if that elephant was still there, he would tell Brenda to shoot.

On the eighth day, my PH had a bout with malaria, so I tagged along with Brenda and her new PH. Yes, we went to the same water hole; and yes there was the very same elephant – highly unusual. Her PH, with over 125 elephant to his credit, couldn't understand why two very experienced professional hunters had passed; and said to Brenda "You should shoot this elephant!"

Elephant are vegetarians, eating only bark, leaves and grass; but they can destroy forests, if overpopulated.

This was our first sighting of this bull, on day one; he was drinking at an underground spring.

A typical 'end of safari' picture. This is what Brenda shot in 21 days of hunting - three of the big four.

We watched from 60 yards as the elephant finished drinking and began walking away. We paralleled him, trying to get out in front and close the distance.

But quite unexpectedly, the bull turned 90 degrees and walked straight toward us. Brenda stood in the middle of the well-worn trail with her gun at the ready, waiting for her PH to give the 'shoot' order. The elephant was 9 steps out when the order came, and he went down with one shot in the brain – and what a great trophy he was.

Luwele Camp | Selous Game Reserve | Tanzania, Africa | 13 December 2003

As the bull walked away, we could see that one tusk was longer than the other.

LEOPARD
in the
SUNSHINE

I swapped the 375 H&H for my Winchester 1895 in 405, as we walked up on the dead leopard.

There was a time, many years ago, when some people thought leopard were nearly extinct; but this was before they came to understand that it was only daylight sightings that were rare – you see, the leopard hunts at night. So this one, in mid-afternoon, was quite unexpected.

We had just descended into the top end of a roadless and dry river bottom, planning to follow it for a few miles looking for buffalo. Lumbering along in the safari car, we came upon a small herd of sable and stopped to watch — more for a break than anything else, as the bull clearly wasn't a shooter. I began looking around and caught a glimpse of what looked like a small lion moving through the scattered brush, about 175 yards behind us. The PH got a quick look also and pronounced that it was a leopard, not a lion – just before it disappeared in the brush.

As the leopard went out of sight, the PH noted that he had a varmint call and asked if he should give it a try. "Of course!", so we bailed out and set up in the shade of a small bush near the safari car. It sounded like the distress call of a rabbit, caught up in some life-ending struggle. We called for only a short while and out of the brush came the leopard. Slowly he walked our way, stopping on occasion and sitting on his hind legs for a few seconds, whenever we would stop calling. When the squealing started back up, he would come again. It was

cat and rabbit for several minutes, as he closed the distance. The safari car was in plain sight and we were concerned, but he was walking straight into the late afternoon sun and the car never caught his attention.

The kill zone on a leopard is probably only six inches wide, as he faces you straight on, so we allowed him to keep coming. I was in the sitting position with the scope on him the whole time and at 125 yards I was comfortable with the shot — the PH gave me the green light. The hold was good and the 300 grain Partition was effective. I swapped the scoped 375 for my open-sighted 1895 Winchester and we walked up to confirm the kill – a leopard in the sunshine.

Luwele Camp | Selous Game Reserve | Tanzania, Africa | 29 November 2003

We were watching this sable when I looked around and saw the leopard behind us.

Brenda and I are still smiling late in the safari, on one of those rare occasions when we left camp a little later than normal, and went our different ways for the day of hunting.

If you've shot a leopard, it's traditional to stop outside camp and fire a couple of rounds into the air. The whole camp shows up and throws you a party.

This is the 'leopard rifle', the first version of The Nearly-Perfect Safari Rifle.

A WOUNDED LEOPARD
– Serious Problem

This is a staged reenactment to show the final position of the leopard, in the red circle.

There is nothing in Africa quite as dreaded as a wounded Buffalo, Lion or Leopard. Nearly all of the recorded incidents of maulings or death to clients and professional hunters are attributed to following up on these three wounded animals. It is for this reason they are called 'dangerous game'. On the other hand, a close counter with a perfectly healthy elephant can and has been equally hazardous.

Putting a killing shot into a leopard should be pretty straightforward, as the distance is typically only 25-40 yards and the client is normally sitting – with a steady rest. However, a leopard usually comes to the bait just before dark and there is often a sense of urgency to shoot, especially if the leopard is nervous.

This leopard was nervous, switching directions on the limb, never lying down to eat and I apparently hurried the shot, hitting him too far forward and out of the chest cavity. We found blood, but now had a wounded leopard on our hands.

Experienced professional hunters prefer to follow-up wounded leopard with a seasoned partner, not the client; because a wounded leopard almost always charges and they come so very, very fast. It is a few kill or be killed seconds, although leopard typically claw and bite everyone in the party, then run back into the bush – which ends the follow-up. A wounded leopard is a serious, serious problem, and no professional hunter looks forward to it.

We returned to the blind about 8:00 am the next morning. Brenda and I stayed with the car while our PHs and trackers started the slow, painstaking follow-up process. For me, reading a good book was the best way to pass this time.

The first shot came without notice one hour and 15 minutes later, from about 400 yards away, with 12 more shots coming so fast they could barely be counted – two Benellis at full throttle. The leopard charged from 45 yards out and died only 3 steps away – all in just over two seconds. Then came the shouts of celebration from the PHs and trackers and we knew immediately of their success.

I can only imagine the adrenalin flowing through the veins of the PHs and trackers during that one hour and 15 minute follow-up, culminating in the last two seconds.

Luwele Camp | Selous Game Reserve | Tanzania, Africa | 6 December 2005

I gathered up the empties and tossed them on the ground, as you see them, just because it seemed that they belonged in the picture.

Here's the leopard hunting crew. I don't deserve much of the credit for this trophy. Note the empty shells in the foreground. PH Jean Louis Masson on the left and PH Fred Blochet next to me – both from France.

PH Fred likes to put a string under the scope. I think that may have affected my shot.

This is the leopard's view of the blind – in the daylight.

BUFFALO on the MOUNTAIN

Bruce, the PH, is pointing at the buffalo on top of the mountain a mile or so away.

As our plane circled to get downwind of the runway, we could see small herds of buffalo on the hills and in the valleys below. This was a seven day hunt in rough country and son Russell, amazed at seeing all the small herds, excitedly exclaimed that he wanted to hunt buffalo all week long and shoot one on the last day. You see, buffalo hunting can be pretty exciting!

The Dande Safari area is communal land, which means that native people live in and around the area – as compared to national forest land where no one lives. It is located along the Zambezi River in north central Zimbabwe. This was a family safari, with Russell and Sara doing the all the hunting and Brenda and I just along for the ride.

There were a good many elephant in the area, but only a few plains game; however, all that mattered to us was buffalo and there were lots of them. One day we saw two young bulls sparring, like a couple of white tail bucks. I have never seen that before or since. Another day Russell and his PH were 50 yards out in front and sat down beside a tree to watch a large herd on the opposite hillside. But then, the herd shifted direction and fed right past them – some within 20 feet; pretty scary!

Nearly noon on the sixth day, a single bull ran across the dirt track about a hundred yards ahead of our safari car. We tracked him for a couple of hundred yards and he was still running, so the PH suggested we go back to the safari car and have our lunch, then start the track on a full stomach.

Lunch was about over when I glassed the hills in the direction the buffalo had gone and saw a lone bull walking up the hill a mile or so away. We looked him over as best we could with 10x40s and Russell said "That's my bull; let's go!" Taking a straight line across the bottom and up the hill, rather than following his track, we caught up to him in a short hour. He was bedded and we were quite close before he jumped and ran. Russell said it was like shooting a rabbit on the sporting clays course; one high shoulder shot from his 500 Nitro Express and this buffalo on the mountain hunt was over.

Dande Safari Area | Zimbabwe, Africa | 11 July 1997

Russell, and PH Bruce, pause for a moment before starting up the mountain.

Russell and his PH congratulate each other over the difficult but successful stalk.

Russell says his Charles Boswell 500 Nitro Express is powerful enough to stop a fight.

A celebration at camp; Russell with cigar and PH with a cup of coffee.

PLAINS GAME
of *Africa*

For reasons only they would know, Professional Hunters in Africa have always divided game into just two categories – dangerous game and plains game. The term dangerous game has always been pretty well-defined (see Section One), and they are what movies are made from; everything else is plains game — it's just that simple.

But there are a lot of animals in Africa that don't fit well under the plains game banner – like hippo, croc, hyena, jackal and ostrich; or some of the small antelope that aren't much bigger than a jackrabbit. However, there has never been another category to put them in, so you will find those stories here.

Also, there's a lot more to a safari than hunting; every day in Africa is an opportunity for a unique experience, no matter what the plan. Often, if the trophy collecting is ahead of schedule and there's a little extra time, allowing yourself the opportunity to explore a petrified forest, an ancient vine, a special land formation or walk elephant trails — that perhaps no human has ever traveled — is a very special treat. You'll find stories like that here also.

The
DEAD
WILDEBEEST
That Stood Up

Brenda with the wildebeest; what an unusual picture - he almost looks alive.

The safari car was coming in for the evening, just at last light, when they spotted a lone wildebeest bull, standing broadside about 200 yards off to the right. As Brenda needed leopard bait, she and the PH bailed out and found a good spot to shoot from; the sticks were set up and she took the shot – the bull ran off deeper into the bush and out of sight. With flashlights in hand, everyone walked to the spot where the bull had been standing and flashed around looking for blood; but they found none. Finally, the PH announced that the shot must have been a bit high and a clean miss, so the group loaded back into the safari car and continued on to camp. That's the way the story was relayed to me around the campfire that evening.

At 6:00 a.m. the next morning, as we were ready to leave camp, our PHs asked if we wanted to go our separate ways, or join forces and spend a few minutes looking for the wildebeest bull of last evening. I looked at Brenda; she simply said that it was a good hold and she should have hit it. So, since it was near, we decided to both go back and double check.

Over dinner the previous evening, we had discussed that even if we were able to find the wildebeest, the hyenas would likely have found it during the night and there wouldn't be a strip of meat or hide on its bones. "Nothing lasts overnight in the bush," the PHs said!

It was a short drive and walk; and with two sets of trackers and Brenda's confidence in the shot, I wasn't surprised when they immediately found the blood they hadn't been able to see with flashlights the night before. Dried blood is a lot harder to see than fresh blood, but we slowly tracked about three hundred yards and there was the dead wildebeest – and he was completely untouched by the predators.

But the most interesting thing was that the wildebeest was lying flat on his left side, with legs locked in the extended position and his head turned slightly to the right.

Since he was completely stiff, it wasn't possible to get him into the traditional trophy position, so we simply stood him up and took these pictures.

Luwele Camp | Selous Game Reserve | Tanzania, Africa | 21 August 2001

Leopard bait; a wildebeest quarter is often used for leopard hunting.

Brenda and her hunting team. Since the wildebeest looks alive, they are pretending to wrestle with it.

This wildebeest fell near an anthill, so we took this picture just as he fell.

Brenda and a black wildebeest from a Botswana safari.

MAMBAS & PUFF ADDERS
Two Killer Snakes of Africa

He came out of the forest on the right side of the track and raced quickly across the dusty road to the far side; but then he made the last mistake of his life – he stopped. Our safari car was cruising along a narrow dirt track at about 30 kilometers per hour, with thick bush on both sides. There was only one view — straight ahead. The trackers started yelling "nyoka", "nyoka", "nyoka"; which for me translated into "hey, there's a big snake crossing the road in front of us." I grabbed my rifle, stood up and tried to figure out what all the commotion was about – all at the same time.

We came to a complete stop about 20 yards from this huge black mamba, as I bolted a round into the chamber. He was now coiled up and trying to hide in light grass on the left side of the road, but still very visible to us. Likely my bullet never actually touched the snake; a 400 grain projectile, coming from a 416 Remington Magnum, works like a small mortar when it hits the sandy soil – close is good enough, and the results were fatal.

Now, from my perspective as a safari hunter, the concern about dangerous snakes in Africa is a bit overrated. Yes, there are poisonous snakes there; and yes, many natives get bit and die each year; but in my experience, on safari you will be lucky to see a snake.

There are two reasons for this; first, snakes apparently have the sense that they are at the bottom of the food chain; hyenas and leopard eat them and elephant step on them. It should be no wonder that when they hear the leaves or grass rustle – or the ground vibrate, most of them will get out of the way very quickly. Second, the trackers and the professional hunter are almost always in front of you when you're on track in the bush.

I feel fortunate to have seen several mambas in Africa and they have almost always been on the move — going the other way. Puff adders, on the other hand, have never been on the move, but rather have been laying on an elephant trail, catching some sun. This is when I take comfort in the fact that there are trackers and a PH in front of me.

Luwele Camp | Selous Game Reserve | Tanzania, Africa | 30 August 2001

Ten feet is about as long as black mambas get and this one is pretty close.

This is a puff adder, another killer snake. Yes; of course he is dead.

We have hardly ever seen snakes in camp, and then only small ones; but spiders, ants and scorpions are often commonplace.

It's easy to spot a snake as he is crossing the road; the hard part is getting him to stop so you can shoot him.

PH Mauro Fabris holds a dead mamba; these snakes are very fast, but fortunately they are always going the other direction.

39

The NEARLY-PERFECT
Safari Rifle

This is the final version; the scope is a Leupold VX-7, 1.5-6 x 24mm. It feels, functions and shoots as good as it looks.

There's no such thing as 'perfect', so 'nearly-perfect' is about as good as a man can hope for. On safari one year, I got to thinking about what a rifle would have to be to make me really happy – well, it would have to be 'nearly-perfect' – attractive, all the right features and accurate.

At the time, a pre-64 Winchester Model 70 in 375 H&H was my choice; and it certainly is a classic. But, I wanted a rifle that looked better, felt better and shot better; and didn't think that was too much to hope for.

There wasn't much thinking about which caliber was nearly-perfect, the 375 H&H is so tried and proven that it would be an up-hill battle to argue against it; and besides, it was already my favorite caliber for Africa. Choosing the best action didn't take much thought either. In my opinion, the action of a man's dangerous game rifle should be one he is intimately familiar with – most of the guns in my rifle vault have a Remington 700 action. The only functional changes we made to the action were the addition of a three-position safety, welding on a new bolt handle that was longer with a larger and rounder bolt knob, and replacing the trigger with one that is crisp, consistent and adjusted to my preferred weight of pull. A Shilen #4 contour barrel gave us the desired weight and balance, and express sights – in conjunction with QD scope mounts – provide flexibility of sighting options if necessary. We rust blued everything, of course.

In my opinion, a serious rifle stock should be made of English walnut, because it's naturally stronger than black or claro walnut; and to make it nearly-perfect, we installed an all-thread rod down through the grip for additional strength and a hardened steel rod in the forend channel to prevent warping. Glass bedding and pillar bedding are two other hidden features that help keep this wood stock really stable in all weather conditions. Of course, it has an oil finish and checkering we cut entirely by hand.

Since we had a filming studio, it made sense to film the entire project to preserve the idea and all the processes. You can find the videos on the MidwayUSA website or YouTube. For me, this is a Nearly-Perfect Safari Rifle, and it was a lot of fun to build it.

Tholo Safari Camp | Near Ghanzi | Botswana, Africa | 27 August 2011

Some safari cars are set up like this, so your rifle is never out of reach or out of mind.

On two occasions I've taken shots over three hundred yards with this rifle. Both were one-shot kills – this hartebeest and a zebra.

A great picture of the 'first generation' gun. The noticeable differences are the reddish stain on the wood, original bolt handle and safety — and the stainless steel barrel (Tanzania 2005).

This wildebeest was the first animal shot with the second generation Nearly-Perfect Safari Rifle – Botswana, 2011.

LUNCH in the AFRICAN BUSH

In the larger hunting concessions of Tanzania, it's pretty common to be 50 miles or more from base camp at lunchtime. The plan for the afternoon might be to continue on a particular dirt track or be someplace special near sunset. In these large areas, it's almost never convenient to go back to camp at mid-day, so we have lunch in the bush.

Each morning, before our safari car leaves camp, a large wooden lunch box is loaded into the back. It's stocked with cooking equipment, utensils and enough fresh and canned food to provide lunch — and an evening meal, should we break-down and get stuck out overnight. Also, there's a portable table and collapsible chairs – just about everything for a nice relaxing meal.

The lunch box is divided in half, with one side insulated and holding some meat, salad, freshly-cooked potatoes, rice and pasta. Then of course there's freshly-baked and toasted bread, onions, garlic, tomatoes, perhaps an avocado and some fresh fruit. We never want for anything; there's even a bottle of wine.

Lunchtime is never a scheduled event; it just happens, based on the circumstances of that day's hunt. If there's nothing going on, we normally stop between 11:30 and 12:30; but if we're on a buffalo or elephant track, there's no lunch break. Lunch at 2, 3 or 4 in the afternoon is just as common as mid-day.

The first order of business is to find a good lunch tree. The professional hunters and trackers have favorites of course, since they're familiar with the hunting

This was an early December safari, and it was so hot that we took off our shirts to cool down at lunchtime. PH Nicolas Dubich on the left.

With shade trees on either side, we stopped for lunch right in the middle of the dirt road.

A younger Nicolas frying bananas (with sugar), one of my favorite deserts.

area; but if we aren't close to a favorite tree they just start looking. It must be large, with lots of dense green leaves, to block the sun. The safari car pulls under the tree and the lunch process begins.

The table (complete with tablecloth) and chairs are set up and a small cooking fire is built. The PH serves as the chef, preparing everything, but typically delegating the cooking to our driver.

It's all so very good that I have to be careful how much I eat; yes, it's quite possible to gain weight on safari. If lunch is at mid-day, there's usually time for a nap or some reading before we head out about 3:30 or so and hunt back toward camp. Lunch in the African bush is a very special time!

Kibaoni Camp | Selous Game Reserve | Tanzania, Africa | 3 December 2013

SPREAD MY ASHES
in Africa

It's a simple monument, made up of things from the land – Warthog Tusks, Snail Shells, Lucky Beans and Porcupine Quills.

At sunset we erected a simple monument, on the escarpment above camp, overlooking the Mbaragandu River; it was our tribute to Brigitte. We spread her ashes on the ground, covered them with sand; and added warthog tusks, snail shells, lucky beans and porcupine quills – all staples of the African bush. Then we toasted to her memory with French Champagne and said our last goodbyes.

Brigitte Klineburger, wife and partner of the famous international hunter Bert Klineburger, was a dear friend of the family and passed away quite unexpectedly in June, 2013.

She spent a considerable amount of time in Africa, first as a safari operator in the C.A.R. with her husband Bert and later as a booking agent. My wife and I enjoyed the company of Brigitte and Bert on two different safaris in Tanzania and a couple of fishing trips to Alaska. She was a joy to be with.

Africa is a mysterious place, in terms of the impact it has on the human mind. Dr. David Livingstone spent much of his life there (in the mid-19th century), in search of the source of the Nile River. He died in Africa, but made plans for his body to be returned to England for burial. It's said today that before one begins the long flight home, from the first trip, they begin planning their return. So, I guess it isn't surprising that someone would have a last request to 'spread my ashes in Africa'. Interestingly this is the second time Brenda and I have been asked to do just that.

Many years earlier Brigitte had sent Brenda a poem called The Exile. Following are the last two verses:

Oh! How I long to lie by a rivers edge
One starry velvet night.
There let me dream of days gone by
Until my soul takes flight.

Then should I wake in Africa
I'll hear the Bul Bul's song.
And know that I am home again,
Back home where I belong.

When the news came of her death, we were just five months from our scheduled safari to Africa; that Brigitte had booked for us. It was her husband Bert who suggested we spread some of her ashes in Africa, as she would have wanted that – and so we did!

Kibaoni Camp | Selous Game Reserve | Tanzania, Africa | 14 December 2013

This was not the sunset on the day of our ceremony, but was grand enough to take a picture.
Visitors to Africa always talk about the beautiful sunsets and this was one of them.

Fires burning on either side of the monument – at sunset.

Professional Hunters, Clients, Trackers and Staff say goodbye to Brigitte.

Russell is a little over six feet tall, so this a pretty big croc.

The dirt track ran generally along the side of the riverbed, through intermittent brush, and occasionally provided a great view of whatever pools were still holding water during the dry season. As the safari car came upon one of the view points, the trackers spotted a big crocodile sunning on a sandbar several hundred yards down and on the other side of the river. Although Russell wasn't hunting croc, this was a big one and it was a quick decision, between he and the Professional Hunter (PH), to go for it.

"Be very quiet and keep low; crocs can see and hear very well"; this is the typical advice from a PH when trying to get a client close enough take a shot – and I mean close. When a croc is near the water, you always shoot for the brain, which is pretty small — perhaps the size of a walnut. You must get close enough to hit the walnut from whatever makeshift rest you can set up, or the croc runs to the water and is gone in seconds.

As elephant hunting was Russell's primary interest, he had removed the scope from his rifle several days earlier, after sighting in. Not a problem, the Leupold quick-detachable rings and bases are very precise; he slipped the ring studs back into the bases, tightened the levers, and off they went.

At 75 yards, they ran out of cover; Russell stretched out prone, peeking over the river bank through the scope and took the shot. It was well-placed and the croc hardly moved.

Now, the nervous system on an ancient, cold-blooded reptile like this croc is a bit complicated – or perhaps it's very simple. I remember cutting the heads off of snapping turtles when I was a kid but the turtles continued to move around for several hours, even without a head and a brain. This croc was definitely dead, with a 400 grain bullet through his brain; and the guys took pictures for fifteen or twenty minutes. The picture taking was completed and everyone was just standing around waiting to load the croc into the safari car; but all of a sudden this reptile stood up on all four legs and urinated in the sand. The trackers went absolutely crazy; and along with Russell and the PH, they scattered everywhere. So this is the story of the croc that wasn't dead – and yes, additional shots were fired!

Luwele Camp | Selous Game Reserve | Tanzania, Africa | 19 July 1999

The 416 Remington Magnum is a relatively modern African big game cartridge. Russell's rifle is a custom-stocked Winchester Model 70.

Russell and his PH pretending to wrestle with the 'presumed dead' croc. The safari car is in the background, across the river.

A pretty big croc and a great picture, with the river in the background.

Which smile is better, Russell's or the croc?

RUSSELL'S Giant HIPPO

This is a really big hippo; Russell is over six feet tall to provide a perspective.

One of the trophies on Russell's wish list was lion, so we were always looking for lion tracks in the dirt roads as we drove around. On occasion a lion will be spotted from the safari car, but normally you find the tracks where they have crossed or walked on the dirt road – and late one morning we did just that. The tracks were large, so we knew they were made by a male, and they were fresh so there was a good chance the lion was nearby. Now we needed some bait to hang in a tree, hoping the lion would find it. Impala is fine for leopard bait, but for lion, we needed something bigger. Buffalo is always a good choice, as are any of the larger antelope; and of course, lions eat hippo. Since we were near a riverbed, the PH asked Russell if he wanted to walk the edge and possibly shoot a hippo for bait. Russell said "sure!"

Now, let me tell you a couple of things about hippos; first, they get very big – up to 6,000 pounds; second, it is said that they kill more people in Africa than lion, leopard, buffalo or elephants – so they aren't to be taken for granted. It requires a cool head and 'enough gun', if you want to hunt hippo out of the water. The river was mostly dry, but there were still a few small pools of water that the hippos used. The PH thought we might find one laying up out of the water in the tall grass, so we began walking the hippo trails through grass way over our heads. The going was slow and quiet. Hippos make very little noise when they're resting, so on this hunt our eyes were more important than our ears.

The line was composed of two trackers up front, the PH then Russell and myself. We followed one track, then another, then another – over the ridges and through the grass; then we heard movement in the grass on the next ridge over. Slowly a huge hippo lumbered into sight – perfectly broadside and just 12 steps away. Russell raised his rifle and fired one shot to the brain.

We had no way to weigh this hippo, but the trackers and PH agreed that they had never seen one bigger; and now, we had lion bait.

Mkuku Camp | Selous Game Reserve | Tanzania, Africa | 30 September 2000

Russell donned a red beret to strike this French professional hunter 'pose'.

Russell's Charles Boswell double in 500 Nitro Express. He used solids on the hippo.

KYNOCH ·500"

The pores in a hippo's skin secrete oil, as we discovered after the fact. Most of it washed out and he wore that same shirt every other day, for the rest of the safari.

The HIPPO That CHARGED

This is a large male hippo, but they get even bigger.

"Do you want to shoot a hippo?" The safari car had stopped, without apparent reason, and this question was put to me by the PH. "Where?" "There, sleeping in the water." "What would we do with him?" "Use him for lion bait!" "Ok, but I'm not going to shoot him, asleep in the water." "No problem, we can make him charge!"

The plan was simple; the PH and I would walk quietly to within about ten steps of the edge of the water; a tracker would proceed forward and throw some sticks. When the hippo woke up he would charge, whereupon the tracker would run back between the two of us. The last instruction from the PH was "don't shoot until all four feet clear the water."

I was armed with an old double rifle in 500 Nitro Express and my PH also had a big double; so there was no concern about being run over by a charging hippo. We got set up, the tracker threw the sticks, the hippo charged, the tracker ran and then it was just the two of us and four rounds of ammo. But the hippo didn't understand the plan. As his front feet cleared the water (about 10

steps distance), he turned 90 degrees and ran away. I never fired!

It was very dry and there wasn't another waterhole, so after a couple of hundred yards, the hippo ran into a small pocket of thick brush. We approached the brush and repeated the earlier process. On the third stick, the hippo charged.

Now was the moment of truth, but frankly I wasn't prepared; as I had given no thought to my aiming point. I put a 570 grain Woodleigh solid right in the middle of his head (six inches below the brain) at about eight steps. He turned to his left and I put the other solid in the middle of the side of his head – still far from his brain. He ran back into the brush and died a few minutes later, from the full-length penetration of the first shot. The lesson I learned from this was critically important — always have a plan for your aiming point on a charging hippo, buffalo or elephant, or you may not live to tell a story like this.

Luwele Camp | Selous Game Reserve | Tanzania, Africa | 28 August 2001

Sunsets in Africa are often spectacular!

They say that hippos kill more natives than any other animal in Africa. These teeth are one of the reasons why. Brenda was with me on this hunt.

Hippo is a preferred lion bait. This hind quarter is being hung on a broken tree in the sand river.

A huge 'wad' of hippo in a horrific mud hole; we are very close and they want to escape, but prefer this to the open ground.

CROCODILE at FIFTY PACES

This is not a huge croc, but in deep water could easily take a medium sized antelope or a human.

"Do you want to shoot a croc?" With that simple, unexpected, whispered question from my professional hunter, this story begins; you see, we were looking for a hippo to shoot for lion bait – and the thought of bumping into a croc never crossed my mind. "Well, I don't know; where is he and how big?" I whispered back. We were walking alongside a dry riverbed, in pretty tall grass, crossing through many ditches that carried water down the river during the rainy season – a decent area for hippo, but not a likely place to find a crocodile.

The croc was about 50 yards to our right, by a small pocket of water that we couldn't see, and the trackers had spotted him as they stepped off the higher ground and into the ditch. I moved forward quietly for a look. All we could see was the middle part of the left side of a crocodile – no head, no tail, no legs; just the middle. He was perfectly broadside, facing left. "Do you want to shoot him?" "How big is he?" "I can't tell, but he's pretty good – perhaps 10 feet." "Ok, I'll shoot him." In hunting, and especially in Africa, shot opportunities often come just that quickly, so one must always be mentally prepared to make a

quick decision – yes or no. This was an unusual situation, as we could only see half of the trophy.

My rifle was an original Winchester Model 1895 in 405 Winchester (made in 1904), plenty of cartridge, but you have to hit a croc just right, or he immediately takes off – into the water, which they are never far from.

We could just see the crease in his skin, behind his left front leg, and the PH said to shoot him there. We were in no hurry; the PH carefully set up the sticks, I settled in, carefully took aim and squeezed the trigger. The croc never moved, and there was no evidence of a hit; so I shot him again – with the same aiming point and got the same results. "He must be dead, let's go see!" Both shots were practically in the same hole and the croc was dead, however we put one additional shot into his brain – just for our peace of mind. He flopped into a small pool of water below.

Mkuyu River Camp | Selous Game Reserve | Tanzania, Africa | 30 September 2000

The trackers tied a rope around his leg and pull him out.

This is the entire pool of water and not much to hide in; but if he were only wounded, it would have been a nightmare to have gotten him out. That's son Russell on the left.

My 1895 with a vintage box of Ammo, however I was using reloads with 300 grain Woodleigh soft point bullets.

A croc could easily hide even in small water like this; I was not the first to cross.

.405 CALIBER, SOFT POINT, MODEL 1895
20

A MILLION YEARS
of Erosion

This pedestal sticks up like a sore thumb, between the escarpment above and the river far below.

Intrigued; that's probably the best word to describe my thinking, when this small pedestal came into view. Our safari car had been climbing steadily for twenty minutes and we were approaching the escarpment that defines the plateau, far above the river. My professional hunter had seen this sight many times before; but, when I asked if he had ever climbed that pedestal, his answer was no. When I asked why not, he offered only that he had never had a hunter who was interested. Well, he did now!

Growing up in Missouri, mountain climbing was never an opportunity, but I have climbed many, many trees and hills. This pedestal looked like a great challenge and a lot of fun. Also, it was the next to the last day of our safari and we were finished with all the serious hunting.

This plateau and drainage system were formed millions of years ago and every year during the rainy season, the escarpment erodes a little or a lot, depending on the intensity of the rains. Apparently this pedestal had been part of a ridge that extended out from the plateau; and the part of the ridge nearest the plateau had eroded away, leaving this pedestal a mile or more out.

The road took us within a thousand yards, after which we parked and walked the rest of the way. The sides were sheer for the last 50 feet, with only roots and tree limbs offering any hope of getting to the top. It was about 100 yards wide and we circled it easily, looking for a better way up – there wasn't one.

We left our guns with a tracker at the bottom, hoping there wasn't any dangerous game on top, and started up. It was an easy climb, for a person of reasonable shape, and soon we were walking the top – and smiling.

It's an interesting feeling to spend time in a place that has been separated from the rest of the world for perhaps a million years. There is some sense of security, like being in a fortress. And some sense of disappointment, knowing that the world is constantly changing and one day this pedestal will have eroded completely away. I put it on my bucket list to return and climb it again.

Kibaoni Camp | Selous Game Reserve | Tanzania, Africa | 14 December 2007

PH Fred Blochet and myself on top.

The sides are sheer. Roots and fallen trees offer the only way to gain access to the top.

For a country kid, who grew up climbing trees, this was just another day outdoors. You can see a tracker at the bottom. Only one of the three would climb with the PH and myself.

This was our first sighting – from many miles distance; within a few seconds we had agreed to climb it.

Like
FATHER
Like SON - Not!

Hard to imagine what Russell was thinking, as he sat patiently and watched them secure the bungee cords to his legs. The body harness is already attached.

We had just finished a wonderful fourteen day hunting safari in northern Zimbabwe and had allowed a couple of extra days at the end to visit Victoria Falls and the nearby town of the same name – just being tourist.

Victoria Falls is considered to be the largest waterfall in the world; it's over a mile wide and 300 feet high – truly majestic, especially during the season of high water flow. It's listed as one of the seven natural wonders of the world – and when you see it, you immediately understand why.

We stayed at the classic Victoria Falls Hotel. This lovely building went up in 1904 and is a designated world heritage site – pretty neat place to visit. That evening, dinner was an outside buffet and I recall having had the opportunity to taste fried grasshoppers and beetles – not exactly what a country boy from Missouri would be thinking about for dinner.

The next day we did some souvenir shopping, and in one of the shops there was a poster advertising bungee jumping off the Victoria Falls Bridge, over the Zambezi River. Our son Russell, 23 years old at the time, immediately lit up with the prospect of such a grand adventure. He insisted that the entire family join him, and especially me; but got no takers.

He bought his ticket and signed a release, then we had to walk across the bridge to the Zambia side to sign another release – after all, the bridge is anchored to the ground in both Zambia and Zimbabwe. Then, we walked back to the middle of the bridge for the jump.

There was quite a long line, all young folks, of course. When Russell's turn came, they carefully secured the bungee cord to his legs; he turned and smiled at us, then off he went. I cannot explain what it felt like when he jumped off the platform and looked four hundred and twenty feet down into the Zambezi River; nor can I explain how comforting it must have felt when the bungee cord worked according to plan. After the bouncing settled down, the crew pulled their Customer back up to the bridge and untied him.

Russell and I share a lot of personality characteristics and have enjoyed many adventures together, but I drew the line on this one, definitely not – like father, like son.

Victoria Falls Bridge | Zimbabwe, Africa | 23 July 1997

The Victoria Falls Bridge, over the Zambezi River, was built in 1905 and connects Zimbabwe and Zambia. It is 420 feet above the river.

That's the Zambezi River below, hopefully farther away than the length of the bungee cord.

Who would want to jump off a perfectly good bridge?

The BURNING of AFRICA

If you like to set fires and burn things up, you're called a pyromaniac – except perhaps in Africa. There, if you burn your thumb flicking matches off the striker strip of a match box and set fire to thousands of acres of tall grass, you're just part of the team; because the annual burning of the grass is one of the grandest side shows of a safari, especially for early season hunters in East Africa.

The rainy season generally comes in late December and runs through March. This is also the hottest time of the year and the grass grows like crazy till the dry season comes. The road crews start the burning process long before the hunting season opens, but generally the grass is too green to burn completely and when the first hunters arrive in July, the burning process continues on up to October – after which the law prohibits further burning as the fires get so hot they can damage the trees.

There are two reasons to burn the grass. First, within a few days of burning, green sprouts come back from the roots and provide a welcome source of fresh grass for all the grazing animals. Second, it's a lot easier to see and track animals after the grass is burned. Interestingly, the fires die out in the cool dampness of the evening air.

Sometimes we set the grass on fire as we walk back to the car after losing an elephant or buffalo track, or finding a 'non-shooter' at the end of the track. Other times we might drive down the dirt roads flicking out matches as we go. We lit this particular fire in the early afternoon, as we left our lunch tree to head out for the afternoon hunt. We were at the intersection of two dirt roads, and none of the four quadrants had been burned, so today we burned the first one.

There is one serious danger when burning and that is the wind. It can shift without warning and you go from upwind to downwind in a matter of seconds. I know of one safari car, complete with guns, that was burned up when the wind unexpectedly changed.

I'm not a pyromaniac, but burning the tall grass of Africa is one of the lasting memories of my safaris there.

Baraini Camp | Selous Game Reserve | Tanzania, Africa | 8 July 2008

We threw matches in the grass on both sides, as we drove the road.

Yes, this is a big fire, but it burns very quickly and doesn't seem to harm the trees — except the dead ones.

They call it elephant grass, because it's tall enough to hide an elephant.

Where there's smoke, there's fire!

A
WARTHOG
in Wild Africa

I have never actually hunted for warthog, but have shot a few. You see, warthog isn't something you go to Africa to hunt, like kudu, sable, bongo or the big five. A warthog is a great trophy, but it is generally an animal you just happen onto while hunting something else; and then, it is simply a question of the size of the tusks and whether taking the shot would interfere with your hunting mission for that day.

This was a strange encounter. We were actually hunting elephant and were on the plateau, above and near the escarpment of the Mbaragandu River Valley in Tanzania. This plateau and river was likely formed by the great East African Rift System that developed 25 or 30 million years ago. We stopped the safari car and walked quietly to the edge of the escarpment to glass the huge area below, between us and the distant river, thinking we might spot something interesting where the bush was thin.

We saw no elephant, but 75 feet below and 150 yards out was a very nice warthog. He was by himself and rooting around in the leaves – completely unaware that we were watching him. Why he was so far from the river with no apparent water supply, we didn't understand. It only took one quick look for me to know he was a shooter, then eye contact with my professional hunter for confirmation. The tracker set up the sticks and I shot him – simple as that.

A very nice warthog, shot with my first generation of the Nearly-Perfect Safari Rifle in 375 H&H.

I cannot tell whether I was half way up or half way down. This was a unique experience in Africa.

But now we had to fetch him out of there, and that turned out to be quite a job. We looked as far as we could see both ways on the rim of the escarpment. Down, nearly straight down, didn't look any easier than where we were, so this was as good as we were going to get. The good news was that a safari car always has lots of rope for tying up baits and building leopard and lion blinds, so we found a good tree to tie to and rappelled to the bottom to collect our trophy. Not too tough; but climbing back to the top, on the same rope, took a whole lot more effort. It certainly was a grand experience and I will never shoot another warthog, without remembering this one.

The shooting 'sticks', common in Africa, are just three pieces of cane secured near the top with a piece of rubber inner tube.

Kibaoni Camp | Selous Game Reserve | Tanzania, Africa | 30 November 2007

Going down was easy, up was a different story.

A GIANT LIZARD
Crawled Between My Feet

I don't know what he was trying to figure out, but apparently he wasn't alarmed.

We had made a nearly-perfect stalk on a pair of warthogs and were standing quietly watching them from about 40 yards distance – already having made the decision not to shoot. Even though the understory was light, they were completely unaware of our presence, and continued to feed, while I took pictures. Then, from about 30 yards off to our left was a rustling in the leaves.

It was a monitor lizard; and he began crawling in our direction. Like the warthogs, he had no idea we were there. Since my camera was already out, I directed it toward the lizard as he continued his approach.

This was a medium-sized monitor lizard, for this part of Africa – about three feet or so in length; but it was a giant lizard to us. The PH was standing a couple of steps to my right and the trackers were slightly behind us. The lizard kept coming, stopping now and then for whatever reason; and I kept taking pictures.

As he got quite close, he turned 90 degrees and continued crawling on a course that would take him right between my feet; ok, so what - it was a lizard, not a cobra. As his head was almost perfectly between my shoes, he must have sensed something wasn't right and he turned slightly to smell my left trouser leg. Apparently the African bush laundry soap didn't cause him undue concern, and he straightened out and crawled out the back side.

Now the dynamics would change. The trackers were just behind me. These guys were from the Maasai tribes in northern Tanzania. While they will

So, does he look like a giant lizard to you? Notice he is sensing the air with his tongue.

We watched these warthogs before and during the lizard encounter. The one on the right has pretty good tusks.

This was the last picture I got before the trackers came unglued.

cheerfully lead you unnervingly close to a Cape buffalo or a bull elephant, they don't have any kind of a tolerance for snakes or lizards. They scattered like a bunch of chickens; the lizard ran off, the warthogs grunted and ran; and we all had a good laugh.

They tell me that the day's activities were quite beyond 'once-in-a-lifetime'; possibly I am the only human being to ever experience and photograph such an event. The African bush is always interesting and sometimes it delivers the completely unexpected. That's one of the reasons I keep going back.

Kibaoni Camp | Selous Game Reserve | Tanzania, Africa | 10 December 2007

COFFEE BREAK
in the African Bush

One of the greatest pleasures of an African safari, for me at least, is the morning coffee break – it's definitely one of the underrated joys of a safari, and I highly recommend it to everyone. There's no set time or place, just somewhere out in the bush; and of course there's no guarantee that you'll even have time for a coffee break, as hunting is always the mission so naturally it takes priority.

In Tanzania, since it's close to the equator, we climb into the safari car and roll out of camp each morning just after 6:00 a.m. My mind starts thinking about a coffee break at 8:30 or 9:00 – unless of course we're tracking elephant or buffalo — or out of the car stalking something we plan to shoot.

Coffee break isn't just about coffee; it's also the opportunity to get a drink of water, take a restroom break and pile on the sunscreen. All these activities generally occur while the coffee is being prepared.

It's almost always my responsibility to request the coffee break and sometimes I even have to insist on it – depending on where the PH wants to go that morning and what time he wants to be there. Sometimes it's cool, but other times, it's quite warm. Based on the temperature, we look for a shade tree or direct sunshine. The driver serves as the official coffee maker; he stops the car in the middle of the dirt track, lowers the tail gate as a makeshift table, pulls out the dry box and whips up our cups of 'high-test' instant coffee. And there are always some cookies, or a piece of cake that the cook has prepared just for this occasion.

I am not a big fan of instant coffee, but somehow it is different in Africa.

Our coffee may be served on the hood of the safari car, other times, we stand at the tailgate; even though we have chairs in the safari car, we never take the time to sit down. I have never counted the number of minutes, but it's probably no more than ten or twelve and we're back on the road, looking for tracks or trophies.

As we get started, I always get out a bag of candy and share it with the team. It truly is a refreshing break; now, I'm good till lunch!

Luwele Camp | Selous Game Reserve | Tanzania, Africa | 19 August 2001

The sun is bright and my PH Fred Blochet and I are standing in the shade enjoying our morning coffee.

It was a cold morning and Brenda and I took our coffee break in full sun. Brenda's is a diet coke; she's not a coffee drinker.

Russell, our son, and I toasting to another great day on safari.

ROBBING
a Honey Tree

This honey tree was in the middle of a sand river. The circle marks the entrance to the bee hive.

We discovered the bee hive quite by accident, while putting the stalk on a zebra in the bed of a dry sand river. This dead tree was serving as our cover when we noticed the bees buzzing over our heads – coming and going from their hive. After shooting the zebra, a plan was made to come back and rob the honey tree – bringing along some plastic containers to hold the honey. Three days later we made it back and proceeded to execute our plan.

It all starts with smoke, which has a calming effect on bees. My dad was a beekeeper, well part-time at least – more as a hobby, you might say. He always had a few beehives out behind the chicken yard, and sometimes on a couple of neighboring farms. Dad would pay my brother Jerry and I fifty cents for each swarm we captured as the colonies were dividing in the summer. We also helped with harvesting the honey, which was an interesting process, and a lot of work. Yes, we got stung a bit, but the pain wasn't unbearable and didn't last long.

My dad made smoke by burning cotton rags, but in the bush the trackers just used sticks and grass. First, they built a fire on the ground, so the wind would carry the smoke to the hive. Then, they made up a wad of dry grass and secured it inside some greener grass. The greener grass served as a handle, and blowing through a hole in the dry grass provided a billowing effect. The trackers made up a second of the 'hand-held' smokers for me, so I could stand close by and observe.

Now it was simply a matter of smoking and hacking with a corn knife till we got to the hollow part of the log, where the bees stored the honey. The trackers reached into the log and pulled out the honeycomb, full of honey.

We ate our fill, chewing and sucking on the comb till all the honey was gone then spitting out the wax and getting another piece. What was left we took back to camp and shared. I do have to say that robbing honey trees is one of my pleasurable memories of hunting in Africa. This time, I got stung only once.

Kibaoni Camp | Selous Game Reserve | Tanzania, Africa | 5 December 2011

The first step is to get a fire started, upwind of the hive.

Working as a team, our trackers smoked the bees and cut open the tree.

There's nothing quite like honey right out of the hive.

One of our trackers holds a small part of the prize; a wax honeycomb full of warm, sweet honey.

To CLIMB a BAOBAB Tree

A giant baobab in the bush of Africa. It is dry season and the leaves have fallen.

It had been a long and successful safari; we had collected most of the desired trophies and were driving around on the dirt roads enjoying the last few days in the bush without a pressing agenda to collect more.

This area has lots of baobab trees and a big one was coming up on our right, about a hundred yards out in the light bush. We stopped the car and walked over to have a look and take some pictures. It's pretty special just being around these big trees. One doesn't have this luxury of time when the hunting is serious, but today it wasn't.

The mass of this tree was awesome, and it was badly scarred from hundreds of years of gouging by the elephants during the dry seasons. The PH, noticing my awe, asked if I would like to climb it. I looked the tree up and down for a moment, turned back to the PH; smiled and said "yes, but how?"

He told me that in Maasailand, where our trackers lived during the off season, honey bees often make their hives up in forks of the branches and the Maasai simply drive sticks into the soft bark of the baobab tree, in order to climb up and get the honey.

So, the trackers used their 'ever-present' corn knives (pangas) to cut a few small pieces of brush and made up some sticks about a foot long, and perhaps an inch across. Then, using the sides of the same corn knives, one of the trackers drove the first stick half way into the side of the tree about three feet above the ground, and another five feet up. The third stick required the tracker to climb onto the first two, which he did; and he then proceeded to climb and drive sticks all the way up to the first forked limbs, at which time the sticks were no longer necessary. The whole process only took twenty minutes, after which the tracker climbed down and I climbed up.

If I ever get lost in Africa and have to spend the night in the bush, now at least I know how to climb a baobab tree to get above the hyenas and lions, or perhaps to look for honey.

Luwele Camp | Selous Game Reserve | Tanzania, Africa | 29 August 2001

The baobab is soft and our tracker easily drives in the sharpened stick.

The trackers had started a fire to burn some grass and it was creeping through leaves toward the baobab when this picture was taken.

This is a giant specimen, approximately 48 feet in circumference and 16 feet in diameter — but they get even bigger.

Once the sticks are driven into place, it's about like climbing into a deer stand.

THE VULTURES OF AFRICA
- After the Kill

The waterbuck carcass is just 15 feet in front of the blind, with the safari car in the rear.

In my experience, vultures are one of the unchanging features of an ever-changing Africa. They cruise around effortlessly in the air currents, all day long, looking for something to eat – generally what's left of an animal that was killed the night before, by one of the land predators. You might think of vultures as the daytime cleanup crew for Lion, Leopard and Hyena.

Although vultures often seem to follow a safari car, you probably won't notice them when you pull the trigger on a trophy animal, but just wait; look into the sky after the pictures have been taken and there will often be hundreds of them – seemingly coming from nowhere. It looks like a slow motion whirlwind, with vultures stacked up into the sky as far as the eye can see.

Depending on the circumstances of your hunt, your need for bait, and the species of your trophy, you may leave the meat in the field and bring back only the skin and horns. If this is the case, by the time you're finished and ready to drive away some of the lower-flying vultures will be landing in the trees.

Now, comes the interesting part. We had just shot a waterbuck and were keeping only the front skin and the horns. The sky was filling up with vultures

and this looked like a great opportunity to get really, really close to them and observe their feeding frenzy; so we constructed a small blind just 15 feet from the carcass. It didn't take much, just a few sticks, some netting and of course the tall grass. We climbed into the blind and the safari car pulled away a few hundred yards. From the perspective of the vultures, dinner was now served.

It took only 20 seconds for the first vulture to land, a few feet from the carcass. In another 20 seconds there were dozens on the ground and one got up enough courage to approach the carcass and take a bite. Then the feeding frenzy began. The carcass and ground around it were covered with vultures.

In 30 minutes, a 500 pound waterbuck was reduced to 50 pounds of bones. Wow; observing vultures up close, just after the kill, is an amazing experience – and only in Africa.

Barani Camp | Selous Game Reserve | Tanzania, Africa | 7 July 2009

The feeding frenzy lasted only about 30 minutes.

The vultures – on the ground and landing. The noise was unbelievable.

Almost immediately after the safari car drives away, the vultures engulf the carcass, each fighting tooth and nail to get his/her part.

If you look up, while taking the trophy pictures, most often you see a sky full of vultures – like this.

ZEBRA!

We think of zebra as just black and white stripes; but study the stripes on the four zebras and you will see that each is different. First generation Nearly-Perfect Safari Rifle in 375 H&H.

White with black stripes or black with white stripes; that idea never crossed my mind when I lined up on his left shoulder and squeezed the trigger. The herd was in a small, burned area, with the male off to the right – and we had quietly made our approach through the tall grass, on hands and knees. I wanted to get within 100 yards, as my rifle had open sights — but at 125 yards we ran out of cover.

It was a kneeling shot; the PH kept the sticks together and stood them on end. I grabbed them with my left hand, laid the rifle across my wrist for support - and took the shot. The zebra dropped in his tracks and the PH exclaimed, "Great shot!"; but I said, "No, if I had hit my aiming point, he would have ran 50 yards." Indeed I had pulled a few inches to the left and hit him in the neck – 125 yards is a long way, with the original sights of an 1895 Winchester.

The zebra is one of the grandest trophies of Africa, whether displayed as a shoulder mount, or made into a rug for the floor or a wall. They all look alike at first glance, but upon closer examination, each has a different pattern to the stripes. Everyone recognizes the stripes of a zebra, but only those who have hunted them understand how great a trophy they really are. Yes, they are abundant in most of the hunting areas of Africa, but are almost always challenging to hunt - because they see and hear so very well.

They are herd animals, typically 6-10 in a group – mares, foals, and one adult male (stallion). Sportsmen only shoot adult males. There isn't much difference in size between males and females; the animals always seem to be shifting about, and it's often a challenge for the PH to pick out the male – except, of course, in those instances when it's possible to view them from behind.

People who have never hunted zebra tend to think of them as domesticated horses and can't imagine why anyone would want to shoot one. Actually, they are part of the horse family, but are very wild and don't lend themselves to domestication. For me, hunting zebra is one of the many reasons I go back to Africa.

Mkuyu River Camp | Selous Game Reserve | Tanzania, Africa | 26 September 2000

The legendary Bert Klineburger was with me on this hunt – December 2007.

This is the zebra of the story, taken with my Winchester Model 1895 in 405 Winchester.

I was with Ryan Fischer, when he shot this Burchell's Zebra in Botswana – August 2011.

FIRST SAFARI
in Africa

It was a typical 'first safari', nine days of plains game hunting with a standard package of trophy animals, and options for many others. But for me it certainly wasn't typical, as I never fired a shot – however, that was the plan from the beginning. Understanding that there would be a time when our kids would be engaged with their own families, and not available to hunt with mom and dad, Brenda and I planned this 'first safari' for the kids – Russell and Sara. Well they weren't really kids; they were 19 and 17 years of age and had both been hunting for ten years, with lots of whitetail deer, prairie dogs and jack rabbits to their credit.

Impala is often the first trophy a hunter takes in Africa. Brenda, with our daughter Sara.

The six hour drive from the airport to the hunting ranch, in a right-hand drive Lincoln Continental, was an unbelievable experience; there weren't many cars, but people were walking everywhere on both sides of the road, and often the women were carrying large baskets of goods or bundles of wood on their heads.

There were two safari cars (Toyota Land Cruisers), each with a Professional Hunter (PH) and a team of trackers; every day Brenda and I would switch cars, so we had an equal amount of time with each of our kids.

Impala, warthog, zebra, duiker, bushbuck, kudu and wildebeest – for each hunter — were all part of the package and none of us had ever seen any of these animals in the wild. The most-difficult of all the trophies was the zebra, as they tended to stay in the brush and stand-off at two to three hundred yards or so — and didn't stand still very long. Russell took a long, hurry-up shot at one and we tracked it for several hours before getting the final shot. I remember commenting to the PH that the zebra was losing a lot of blood and he responded that the wounded zebra could go two or three days losing that much blood – wow! The African animals are often much more difficult to kill than a whitetail deer, especially when marginally hit.

Besides the hunting, I have vivid memories of the multi-course dinners, hot tea at the tent door with our wake up call, the skinning shed, baobab trees, hippos in the water and Victoria Falls. It was a memorable first safari in Africa, and I never even fired a shot.

Nuanetsi Ranch | Zimbabwe, Africa | May 1993

In the winter, with the leaves off, the baobab tree looks like it is upside down – roots on top.

The bushbuck gets his name because he hangs around the bush areas, rather than the open plain. Russell is pleased with his trophy.

When hunting Africa, every day you are outside till dark and often get to see sunsets like this.

Any safari to Zimbabwe should include a side trip to Victoria Falls, considered to be the world's largest waterfall

JACK and the BEANSTALK

This is the trunk of the vine. One of our trackers is on the ground and another climbing. This is one enormous vine.

Everyone knows the fairy tale about Jack and the Beanstalk; but, let me tell you that I have been there and actually seen and touched the beanstalk — and no longer believe it to be a fairy tale. Jack didn't actually cut it down; or if he did, it grew back — because today it's alive and well – in Africa.

We left a dry riverbed and drove into the small circle of trees nearby, to have lunch. There it was — this enormous vine; the first thing that came to my mind was the story of Jack and the Beanstalk, as this was larger than any vine I could ever imagine. Surreal is a word that a country boy from Missouri wouldn't find opportunity to use very often, but I used it on this occasion. It means something like: 'this can't be real', 'it's beyond logic', 'beyond anything my mind can comprehend'. The main arms of the vine were hanging on the trees under the canopy, sometimes spanning 150-200 feet between supports – impossible!

There was no ground cover in this forest, as the canopy was very thick during the growing season – shutting out the sunlight; and the mature trees were sparse inside, making it easy to see the multi-trunked base of the giant vine about 40 yards from where we parked the safari car.

This patch of forest was perhaps 250 yards in diameter; walking around under the canopy, the vine extended in every direction – all the way to the top and edges of this small circle of trees; and the total mass of trunks and arms must be some kind of a world record. The PH told me they discovered the vine while tracking an elephant through this small forest a couple of years back. It was now their favorite lunch place when hunting in this area.

We had lunch and rested for a couple of hours before departing the forest and hunting our way back toward camp. During that time, I began to understand;

I just had to climb this vine, or it would be on my bucket list forever.

Grape vines are some of the oldest living things on the planet, and this is one old grapevine.

Notice how open it is under the canopy and how the vines are mostly unsupported. The safari car is parked directly under the vine.

this was Africa and Jack's beanstalk had obviously been there for a long, long time. It had outlived the trees that it had grown on in its early years and was now supported by the second or possibly even a third generation of trees. Jack may be long gone, but his beanstalk is still there.

Selous Reserve | Mkuyu Camp | Tanzania, Africa | 4 December 2011

This picture provides a good perspective; remember, I am 40 yards from the trunk of the vine.

THE HISTORY of MidwayUSA

Personally, I've always liked reading about history – the history of wars and civilization, of communities and organizations — and the biographies of historic people. Each of us makes history during our lifetimes, at some level, though we don't likely think much of it at the time or feel it important enough to write down for future generations. Perhaps the world would be a better place if we did.

An organization like MidwayUSA, with 38 years of history, has a lot of stories to tell — and some should truly be recorded for the benefit of future generations — either because they're interesting or perhaps because they are historically significant. This section has a few of them.

Every organization has a direction in the beginning – the hopes and dreams of the founders. Then there are the twists and turns of reality that help confirm the initial direction or redefine it as the years go by. Although not intentionally, many of these stories are about me, and how different things have validated or changed my perspectives; I guess the history of Larry is part of the history of the company.

How the
PRAIRIE
DOG
Changed My Life

Devils Tower National Monument

In August of 1971, during a short vacation between college and the Air Force, Brenda and I drove to Devils Tower National Monument, in northeast Wyoming; it was there that I first saw prairie dogs. You could call them cute, but you certainly have to call them obnoxious and destructive, as they were always barking and their dens destroyed the ground for any possible grazing by other wildlife.

Ellsworth AFB, South Dakota, just east of Rapid City and the Black Hills, was my last assignment and my first experience with prairie dog shooting; and wow, for me it was a life-changing event. That part of the country is truly a sportsman's paradise, with plenty of whitetail, mule deer and antelope — plus ducks, turkeys and prairie chickens; and then, there's fishing – year round. I enjoyed everything, but what impressed me most was the prairie dog shooting – as I like shooting equally as much as I like hunting.

Now, prairie dog shooting covers four different disciplines – all of which I enjoy. First is buying guns; then a little gunsmithing to make them more accurate and keep them shooting; of course lots of reloading to make things more affordable; and last, pulling the trigger – learning to judge distance and the wind. There is a lot of opportunity to learn in all four of these disciplines.

My first prairie dog rifle, in the fall of 1974, was a Husqvarna 1950 in 270 Winchester. Actually, this was my deer rifle, but it was all I had; and it only took one afternoon to realize this wasn't a prairie dog rifle. My buddy was shooting a Remington 721 in 222 Remington, with a 10 power Weaver scope – which seemed to be a pretty good rig; the 223 Remington hadn't really 'launched' at that time. I also had a S&W Model 39 in 9mm, which I used a bit for close work, but learned to prefer a revolver over a semi-auto for prairie dogs.

After service, I hunted a few more times in South Dakota, but then switched to the area around Medicine Bow, Wyoming, which was a little closer with more prairie dogs.

Through the years, I bought and sold many rifles, pulled the trigger thousands of times, did a fair bit of gunsmithing and lots and lots of reloading. Unquestionably the prairie dog changed my life.

Medicine Bow, Wyoming | June 1996

The white-tailed prairie dog is a prolific breeder and plays havoc on the western grasslands.

This interesting old building was likely to accommodate the cowboys tending the remote cattle herds, before gravel and blacktop roads and pickup trucks made access quicker and easier.

A view of Devils Tower from the air – west side in late afternoon.

This baby antelope lay perfectly still, until we were only a few steps away; then he jumped and ran.

Larry in a prairie dog field with a S&W M-28.

How The CLAY PIGEON Changed My Life

Clay pigeons have been around since the 1880s. They are a marvel of simplicity, and sometimes durability.

Were it not for my introduction to the clay pigeon, this story couldn't have been written; and possibly I wouldn't even be involved in the shooting sports industry.

Growing up in Marion County, Missouri, I don't recall ever having seen a clay pigeon, though we did have real pigeons in the barn; so my first glimpse was upon moving to Columbia, to attend the University of Missouri. Tigertown Trap and Skeet Club was located in the coal-mining strip pits, just north of town and a fellow student from back home invited me to shoot skeet one afternoon. I was hooked immediately; and apparently for life. Skeet shooting burns a lot of ammo and soon thereafter I bought a MEC reloader.

There was this long date with the Air Force for a few years after college and I shot mostly skeet at my bases in Arkansas, Texas and South Dakota. One spring we put a team together and attended the Armed Forces Championships in Colorado Springs. On the first day I shot 100 straight (my first and only in registered competition), using an old Remington 11-48 in 12 gauge. The second day I broke the first 50, then dropped one each in the last two rounds, to finish with a 198 of 200 – that was quite a confidence builder for a young man.

We started the business in 1977 and it was a very busy time for the next ten years. The British game of sporting clays made its way to America and what a grand game it has been. We sponsored the Louise Mandrell and Charlton Heston celebrity shoots for a few years in the '90s and got to meet and shoot with movie stars like Charlton Heston, country singers like the Mandrel sisters and too many politicians to keep track of.

Since my introduction to the clay pigeon, I've had the opportunity to introduce many, many people to shooting – most importantly my wife and children and MidwayUSA Employees. In 2007, Brenda and I started the MidwayUSA Foundation, with a sole mission of helping to fund high school and college shooting teams, mostly shotgun teams, shooting clay pigeons.

So, who can say how much credit the clay pigeon should receive for helping me get where I am today? I don't know, but do highly recommend clay pigeon shooting to everyone. It may just change your life.

The Sporting Clays Range | Midway Farms | Fayette, Missouri | 24 August 2013

In this picture I am smiling, so you know the shooting went pretty well. That's a Browning Superposed in 12 Gauge.

On this day on the skeet range, my shotgun is a Perazzi 20 gauge.

On the skeet range with a Remington 870, in 1991.

Many of today's traps hold a case or two of birds and are battery operated, like this one.

ONE HUNDRED STRAIGHT

The ammunition companies have long offered patches like this, so shooters can display their accomplishments. The medal was for first place in 12 gauge 'C' class.

The term 'one hundred straight' only has meaning to a clay pigeon shooter. It may have been coined in the late 19th or early 20th century when clay pigeons and trap shooting were just getting started. Or possibly it was created by skeet shooters after the introduction of the game of skeet in the mid-1920s. In any case, one hundred straight has a nice ring to it and is something that all clay pigeon shooters aspire to achieve.

Aircraft gunners in World War II were taught how to shoot down enemy planes by practicing with shotguns shooting clay pigeons. On the skeet range, some clay pigeons require more lead than others, based on the angle of the flight of the pigeon in relation to the shooter. Skeet shooting had been around for fifteen years before World War II broke out and someone decided that learning to shoot skeet would help gunners shoot down enemy planes; what an innovative idea.

After the war, active duty military personnel continued to shoot on the skeet ranges for recreation; and returning GIs built skeet ranges in their hometowns. Unquestionably the adoption of skeet shooting as training for aerial gunners was instrumental in helping grow participation in this sport in the 1950s and 1960s.

The Armed Forces Skeet Championship was created about 1960, and in the spring of 1975 I made my first and only appearance. Stationed at Ellsworth AFB in South Dakota, there was a group of us who shot skeet regularly at the local Elks club. One of our

If pretty guns broke more targets, this one would be a real winner —
Perazzi MX-20, SCO Grade. A delight to shoot, but more for hunting than skeet.

Remington introduced the 11-48 in 1949 and produced it in 12, 16, 20, 28 and
410, before discontinuing it in 1968. They made over 450,000.

group came up with the idea of making the 500 mile trip from Rapid City to Colorado Springs and shooting as a team in the Championships.

My skeet gun was a Remington Model 11-48 in 12 gauge, with a factory ventilated rib and skeet choke. To save the empties, I had a shell catcher clipped to the ejection port on the right side. This gun functioned well, had good weight-forward balance and was one of the premier skeet guns before the introduction of the Remington 1100 in 1963. The shoot was a 200 bird event, 100 each day, and I strung four perfect 25-bird rounds together on day one – 100 straight. The second day started out the same, with two straight rounds; but then I dropped one bird in the third round and one in the fourth – to finish with 198/200 — the best skeet shooting I had ever done.

Armed Forces Skeet Championships | Ent Air Force Base | Colorado Springs, Colorado | Spring, 1975

Briley thin wall choke tubes put an old Browning
Superposed back on the range.

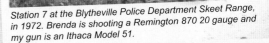

Station 7 at the Blytheville Police Department Skeet Range,
in 1972. Brenda is shooting a Remington 870 20 gauge and
my gun is an Ithaca Model 51.

This is the 'big' Tulsa Gun Show. I'm standing on the upper level (8 acres) with the lower level (4 acres) in the background, and holding a Winchester 101 in 28 gauge.

How
GUN
SHOWS
Changed My Life

A friend once introduced me as having a PhD in Gunology. Of course there is no such degree; but if there was, possibly I would be a candidate — and one of the principle reasons is my having attended a great many gun shows, through the years.

My first show was in Rapid City, South Dakota, in the spring of 1975, while stationed at Ellsworth AFB. Frankly, at that time, I didn't know there were so many models of Winchester lever action rifles. Since that first show, I've had the opportunity to attend the Ohio Gun Collectors Show, the Louisville Show, the Las Vegas Antique Arms Show, the Kansas City National Show and of course my favorite of them all the Tulsa Gun Show, put on by Joe Wanenmacher.

So, what's to learn at a gun show that could possibly change one's life? Well, consider this; at a gun show – especially a large one – there are literally thousands of guns on display (for instance, in March of 2006, we did a pretty scientific estimate of the total number of guns on display at the Tulsa Gun Show and came up with 44,000); also, the man behind the table will likely be very knowledgeable about his guns and happy to share that knowledge with you; and finally, you're allowed to handle almost anything – with permission, of course.

While I've learned a lot about guns at gun shows, a great deal of my learning has been at home, after having made a purchase. First would come a thorough cleaning and inspection, then shooting the gun, studying it and reading every book I could find. Also, there's been a lot of opportunity for gunsmithing and reloading for the guns I've brought home.

This Winchester 101 in 28 gauge didn't appear to have ever been shot, until it found its way into my collection.

My interests continued to grow through the years, to include guns made by Winchester, Remington, Smith & Wesson, Colt, WWI and WWII military arms, black powder cartridge rifles – plus side by side shotguns, and lots more.

So, what's all of this gun knowledge worth practically, and what more will a PhD in Gunology and a dollar buy than a cup of coffee? In my case it's provided a great deal of credibility with Customers and Employees, helped with product development, and opened a lot of doors in the shooting sports industry that may have otherwise remained closed. Gun shows have definitely changed my life!

Tulsa Gun Show | Tulsa, Oklahoma | 6 April 2013

At the big gun shows, there are racks of guns, tables of guns and often stacks of guns – something for everyone.

The History of
MidwayUSA
Part 1

I'm firing a Thompson/Center Hawken in the Black Hills of South Dakota - Summer of 1976

High noon, on the 18th of June was 'opening day'; but it took a lot of planning and hard work to get there. The idea of a gun shop came during the spring of 1976; there was just a year left on my Air Force hitch, and it was time to start thinking about a job. In 1972 I had obtained a Federal Firearms License (FFL) and transferred it from one duty station to the next; buying, selling and trading a few guns.

Hunting and shooting were favorite activities during my teenage years; in my twenties, organized and competitive shooting, gun collecting, reloading, bullet casting and gunsmithing were added to the list — so, starting a gun shop was just a matter of turning my hobbies into a job. That happens often in the shooting sports industry; but 'love of the game' is not a complete recipe for success.

Brenda was supportive and in the summer of 1976 we invited my brother Jerry to join in as an equal partner. He researched the business prospect of establishing the gun shop along the Missouri River between Kansas City and St. Louis. Columbia was his recommendation; since that was home for Jerry and his wife, and Brenda and I had lived there before the Air Force, it was an easy choice.

Needing a name, we came up with Ely Arms, Inc. — after Ely, Missouri (hometown for Jerry and I) – population 26, before we left. We had $30,000 in equity (cash and guns) between us, and found a bank that would loan us another $50,000. Many banks said no, but it only takes one.

We bought 16 acres just west of town, planning to build the gun shop on the frontage and our houses in the back. However, we couldn't get approval from Planning and Zoning, so we bought an acre of commercial property next door – this put us a bit behind schedule. When Brenda and I, with the kids, arrived on May 13, 1977, the building site had been leveled – that was it; but 36 days later we opened for business.

It was a pole-frame, metal building, 32' x 48' (1536 square feet). To save money, Jerry and I did a lot of the interior work ourselves. It was a busy, busy 36 days and that's Part 1 of the History of MidwayUSA – from idea to 'opening day'.

At the Gunshop | 7450 Old Highway 40 West | Columbia, MO | 18 June 1977

This is a publicity photo taken February, 1975, while I was a 2nd Lieutenant, assigned to the Hospital Squadron at Ellsworth AFB, South Dakota.

Brother Jerry, in his Army uniform, about 1969.

Moving Day, 12th of May in '77. That's son Russell, at the curb – not quite 3 years old.

Looking closely, you can see that the name Midway was painted over the original name of Ely.

How I Learned GUNSMITHING

During the GunTec filming years, we built a Nearly-Perfect Safari Rifle from start to finish — truing up the action through finishing and checkering the stock.

Gunsmithing, at its most basic level, is simply the thoughtful use of hands, eyes and brain to disassemble and reassemble a firearm, and to shape and finish wood and metal parts – but how does one learn to do those things? My library has over 100 gunsmithing books; I've read them all, but you can't learn gunsmithing by reading books or watching videos – you gotta do it, with your own hands, eyes and brain.

Just after we opened the gunshop in 1977, a young man walked in and asked if we needed a gunsmith. Since we'd had many gunsmithing inquiries, a deal was made for the Company to buy the equipment and provide counter services – while the "new gunsmith" did the bench work.

The relationship didn't last long; we had the equipment and Customers' guns, but no gunsmith. That's when I started learning gunsmithing – polishing and bluing metal, installing recoil pads, opening magazine wells and ejection ports on 1911s, installing red ramps and white outline sights on S&W revolvers, plus cleaning and general repairs.

We discontinued gunsmithing services in 1979 and except for minor work on personal guns, I did no serious gunsmithing for the next 25 years; but then we decided to create a 'first class' stock refinishing kit. The first thing was to identify the best materials and processes, and the only way to do that was to start refinishing gunstocks. I did sixteen in total – mostly single shot .22 rifles, experimenting with all kinds of finish remover, sandpaper, stock sealer and filler, finishes and polishing materials. You can learn a lot if you refinish that many stocks.

Next we needed a checkering kit, but I didn't know how to checker. Checkering isn't difficult, but learning to checker was my most frustrating learning experience. The breakthrough was learning to hold the checkering tool like the back end of a pool stick – just pushing, not guiding, and applying about the same amount of downward finger pressure as I do on my razor, when shaving.

The GunTec filming years from 2005 to 2012 were a great learning experience. I had two good gunsmithing teammates, Ryan Fischer and Bob DeWitt. We would choose filming topics based on what we wanted to teach our viewers, rather than what we knew how to do; so, before we filmed some projects, we had to do them once for ourselves and then once for the camera.

GunTec Filming Studio | MidwayUSA | Columbia, Missouri | December 2012

Often careful disassembly and cleaning will get a gun back into shooting order, as in this J. D. Dougall percussion double.

Final assembly of a Winchester Model 21, converted from pistol grip to straight grip stock, with the stock refinished, checkering extended and trigger guard straightened and lengthened.

First pass on the master lines is an early step in the checkering process.

The best way to learn gunsmithing, in my mind, is to start with wood and advance to metal – before and after Winchester Model 67 stock.

The 8MM NAMBU Project

The Nambu Type 14 was the principle sidearm of Japanese troops in WWII.

George Spence was a locksmith at Blytheville AFB, Arkansas, when I arrived there – right out of basic training — in November of 1971. A few months later there was a Q&A, in one of the gun magazines, on where to get ammunition for a WWII Japanese pistol; and the answer was 'George Spence, 203 North Main, Steele, Missouri' – Steele was only about 12 miles north of Blytheville, just across the state line. Well, I didn't need any ammunition for a Japanese pistol, but did relish the opportunity of meeting someone who was to me a celebrity, as I had read his name in print in a gun magazine – so I called George and gladly accepted the invitation to visit his shop.

He was 41 years my senior; and in addition to being a locksmith, he had a side business of loading obsolete ammunition — including the 8mm Japanese Nambu pistol cartridge. George and I got along great and I spent quite a bit of time in his shop over the next two and a half years – learning many things about guns and reloading. At the time, I didn't have a clue that meeting George Spence, and other events that would occur later, would help define my career and significantly impact the shooting sports industry.

The process George used to make 8mm Nambu ammunition was very interesting! He started with fired 38 Special M41 military cases and used a hand-operated copper tubing cutter, with a stop added, to shorten them to Nambu length — while he watched television at night; pretty clever. The next step was at his lathe, where he reduced the diameter of the rim slightly and cut in an extractor groove. A friend had made him a carbide die to reduce the neck from 38 special to 8mm (.357 bullet to .323 bullet) and form the shoulder. The only problem with his formed cases was that the head diameter was only .376 and 8mm Nambu chambers are designed for ammunition with a head diameter of .412 – so some of the cases would split when fired. George's position on this was simple "upon firing, some will split; if they do, no problem; if not, they're reloadable." Personally I doubt if any were ever reloaded. He cast lead bullets from a Hensley & Gibbs four cavity mold and lubed and sized them in an old Lyman 45 lubrisizer. I bought a box of this ammo for my cousin Charlie Maple from St. Louis, who had a Nambu pistol, and he and I shot a couple of magazines through it one Sunday afternoon.

When we started the gun shop in 1977, one of the guns my brother Jerry put in as part of his equity was an old Remington Model 8 in 25 Remington. This was a decent, collectable gun, but it was still sitting on the rack that fall when we got a sale flyer from Hodgdon that included some surplus 30 Remington police ammunition at $2.00 for a box of 20. Being a pretty serious handloader, I had George Nonte's book, *The Home Guide to Cartridge Conversions*, and knew that we could make both 25 Remington and 8mm Japanese Nambu pistol cases from 30 Remington; so we bought everything they had (about 10,000 rounds), and got started. George Spence was 70 by this time; he was retired but still making ammo, and was kind enough to loan us his Hensley and Gibbs bullet mold – encouraging me to "go man go!" Thinking about forming the necks the same way that George had, we inquired about a custom die with Frank Snow at Carbide Tool and Die in Covina, CA. He reminded us we could get steel forming dies from RCBS, that would work just fine, and suggested that we talk with Starline Brass, which was located nearby at the time. (More about that later.)

Now having all the tooling lined up, we pulled the bullets and dumped the powder, creating a couple large buckets of primed 30 Remington Brass. Not having a lathe, only a drill press, and needing an efficient method of shortening the cases to Nambu length, brother Jerry came up with the idea of using a 41 Caliber Lyman bullet mold to grip the 30 Remington brass – the lube groove fitting nicely into the extractor groove of the case. A two inch slotting saw and arbor was recommended and supplied by older brother Marion, who was an engineer. Now, gripping the case in the bullet mold and carefully sliding the mold through the jaws of the vise on the drill press, with the arbor spinning the cutoff saw, we completed this first step in the Nambu project – shortening the cases.

The RCBS form dies created the neck, though with considerable effort, as the brass was quite thick and hard that far down on the case; however, they looked great! The case walls around the bullet were too thick of course, but RCBS also supplied a reamer to open the neck to the correct diameter. Then, we cast and lubricated the bullets and loaded the ammunition – using cousin Charlie's

The original Japanese military ammo and the MidwayUSA ammo featured a three-position 'stab' crimp to secure the bullet.

George Spence made his cases from 38 Special cases (left), while the early Midway cases were made from 30 Remington (right). In the middle are Japanese military and MidwayUSA.

This is the original arbor and sawblade used to shorten the 30 Remington cases to 8mm Nambu length, back in 1977.

Nambu pistol to work up the loads. We advertised in Shotgun News and the interest was quite gratifying; everything was soon sold out.

The old NSGA show was in Chicago in 1978 (The S.H.O.T. Show wasn't created till '79). I walked up to the Federal Cartridge booth and pitched them to make us a run of 8mm Nambu brass. They declined, but walked me over and introduced me to Jim Bell at Brass Extrusion Laboratories, Limited; a company that specialized in making brass for obsolete cartridges. At the B.E.L.L. booth I found Jim to be a very friendly and optimistic fellow, and he made it clear right away that they would be delighted to make us some Nambu brass, so we wrote a contract for 500,000 cases to be delivered six months later. This was my first lesson about lead times and delays in manufacturing schedules. The cases began arriving in March of 1980, only eight months behind schedule.

We had started advertising in July, expecting the first deliveries in August and had a considerable quantity of backorders when the first cases arrived in March. To compound things, brother Jerry had decided in January that he wanted to sell his half of the company and move back to the home area and buy a farm. He left in March, just after having set up the newly acquired Dillion RL-1000 machine on which the Nambu was to be loaded.

Hornady made the full metal jacket bullets for us. I personally specified the weight of 102 grains and diameter of .320, without a cannelure – to be true to the original specifications. In retrospect, they probably should have been about .325 and cannelured – for best results. In early testing, I found some of the bullets would push back when hitting the feed ramp and that the accuracy was terrible. Working with Hornady, their tool room made us a 7/8" x 14 collet die with a three-point stab crimp to secure the bullets in the neck of the case, as the last die in the tool head. This also held the bullet long enough for the pressure to build and expand the bullet to fill the grooves in the rifling. Accuracy was fine after that.

Another problem to solve with the Nambu project, was the cartridge box. I liked the Winchester Styrofoam tray and the Winchester folks were kind enough to provide the name of the plant that made them. As it happened, Winchester had a density specification for these trays; during mold changes and shift start up,

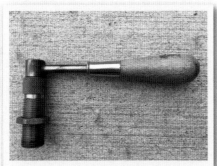

This is the original RCBS bullet puller used to pull the bullets on the 30 Remington ammunition, in 1977. The handle is from a Star lubrisizer, and welded on, to provide a more comfortable grip.

Hornady custom built this 'stab crimp' collet. I drilled a hole in the base of the Dillon press and inserted a short steel rod to stop the downward movement of the collet. A die body forced the collet closed, creating the stab crimp.

This box was made in 1979 or '80, before the name was changed to MidwayUSA.

the plant produced a lot of trays that were not dense enough for Winchester — so they offered to sell these to us at a very good price. All of the Nambu ammunition was packaged in these trays and we also began selling the trays with plain white boxes in September, 1980. With the success of the plain white cartridge boxes, we then began offering plastic ammunition boxes, which were also a great success.

The first 30 days or so, after the initial delivery of brass, was pedal to the metal. I would arrive at the shop at 5:00 a.m. and load ammunition till 7:00, then walk home for a quick breakfast with Brenda and the kids; then back to the shop and load Nambu till 9:00 a.m. — when it was time to open up the store for business. Russell, our 5-year old, went to school and Brenda and Sara, our 3-year old, would come to the shop and box up the ammunition. During the day, between Customers, I would ship the backorders. Store hours ended at 6:00 p.m. and I went home for a quick dinner, then back to the store to load ammo till 9:00 p.m. With the RL-1000, I could load nearly 2,000 rounds of the unprimed brass per hour, which included filling the primer tubes, systematically weighing the powder charges after each 500 rounds and pulling out three rounds per 1000 for pressure testing – which Hornady did for us.

Back now to the earlier reference to Starline Brass. They had started up in mid-1970s, and had been producing 38 Special and 357 Magnum brass for only a few years when we first made contact. They made no ammunition, only unprimed brass and didn't have a distributor, only O.E.M. accounts. Our first order was for 200,000 357 Magnum cases, bearing the Midway headstamp. We advertised in Shotgun news and began to change the shooting sports industry forever. Starline added more calibers, Winchester began selling us bulk brass in 1984 and Remington in 1987. MidwayUSA is the grandfather of the bulk brass business, and it all got started as a spinoff from the 8mm Nambu Project.

The 8mm Nambu ammunition has all been sold and the Project is part of the history of MidwayUSA — indelibly imprinted in my mind. By itself it wasn't a home run, but the lessons learned and the spinoffs we developed helped change my career and forever change the shooting sports industry.

The First Midway Building | 7450 Old Highway 40 West | Columbia, Missouri | 5 February 2014

1,000 rounds of new Starline 357 Magnum brass – the most important spinoff from the 8mm Nambu Project.

In 1980, there were no cardboard/Styrofoam boxes available for reloaders, so we had these made up.

On a visit to the Starline plant, I also met with a company that made plastic products and had a mold to make 38/357 ammunition boxes. From that single box, we developed an entire line of plastic ammunition boxes that are sold today under the Frankford Arsenal brand.

The History of
MidwayUSA
Part 2

I'm holding a U.S. Springfield Trapdoor, Saddle Ring Carbine in 45/70; you can see some of our display of new guns in the background. (fall, 1982)

It was an amazing 7-1/2 years from the day my brother Jerry and I opened the gun shop, Ely Arms, Inc., in 1977 till Brenda and I closed it just after Christmas in 1984 – to become mail order only, with a new name – Midway Arms, Inc. The business was simple in the beginning; we specialized in the sale of new and used guns, ammunition, reloading supplies and equipment, and handgun accessories – there was only 960 square feet of display space. We sold all the desirable handguns we could get our hands on – Smith & Wesson, Colt and Ruger.

Right away it was obvious that our Customers wanted service – in addition to sales and soon we added a second mission – gunsmithing. Then came the opportunity to add a third mission – reloading 8mm Nambu pistol ammunition — and that created the fourth mission – mail order sales — and more importantly – the link to our future. Brother Jerry was a partner in the beginning, but left in early 1980, to move back to the farm. Shortly after advertising the Nambu ammunition, we received a letter from a law firm in New York, advising that our name Ely was in conflict with their client's trademarked brand Eley ammunition. Not a big problem, but **that letter** caused us to change the name from Ely to Midway.

The mail order business grew very rapidly, thanks to the addition of new, unprimed 357 Magnum brass in 1980, and other calibers thereafter. 1982 was our first building expansion and we doubled our square footage and also began using a computer. We bought and sold over 2,000 of the discontinued

Jonathan Browning Mountain Rifles in 1983. Also, our first simple catalog was published in 1983 – 5,000 copies.

The game changer came in July 1984, when Winchester decided to sell us unprimed cartridge cases. We immediately turned in a purchase order for over $1,000,000 to be delivered in January of 1985. In September, we made the decision to close the retail store after Christmas and use the retail space for storage of the Winchester components. Closing the retail store may seem like a dramatic decision, but the mail order division accounted for 80% of our business and we desperately needed more space.

Part 2 of the History of MidwayUSA lasted 7-1/2 years – from 'opening day', to the closing of the retail store.

7450 Old High 40 West | Columbia, MO | December 31, 1984

That's the original Ely/Midway building -7450 Old Highway 40 West — where we started up in 1977 (32' x 48' [1536 square feet]). This picture was taken years later, after the chain link security fence was removed.

This is an early 1980s photo, taken out in front of the gunshop.

Photo by L.G. Patterson.

CLOSED
Mail Order Only
Thanks
MIDWAY

When the sign maker handed me this sign, he said "Larry, I hope this drives away all your business." (December 1984)

We just kept adding on. The low eave and awning, in front of the parked cars, is the original building.

357 MAGNUM BRASS

It all got started about 1935 when Smith & Wesson and Winchester introduced the 357 Magnum cartridge and the large-frame revolver to fire it in.

Important changes often come from small, unknown companies, rather than large and long established ones; such was certainly the case with the availability of bulk reloading components. It all started with unprimed cartridge brass – and two unknown companies – Midway and Starline.

The chain of events goes like this – in 1969, Sierra Bullets, of Santa Fe Springs, CA, sold out to The Leisure Group, who hired Bob Hayden – a young engineer from the Lake City Army Ammunition Plant in Independence, MO – to run their new company. Paul Knepp and Frank Snow (former Sierra Bullet owners) and Bob Hayden incorporated Starline to make cartridge cases. They started from scratch with surplus arsenal equipment, refurbishing and building their own tooling; first production was 38 Special in 1979, followed by 357 Magnum in 1980.

In late 1980, Midway learned that Starline was looking for someone to distribute their 38 and 357 Magnum brass. For an initial order of 200,000 pieces, Starline would put the Midway headstamp on each case at no extra charge. We placed the order, becoming their first distributor – and also put ads in Shotgun News; the phone rang and the mail came – and our industry started changing.

The brass came packaged in large drums and needed to be repackaged by the 1,000 for sale. We designed and ordered the boxes, then bought an electronic scale for $1,800 — pretty new technology in 1980. Finding the source of the cases, ordering boxes, buying an electronic scale, creating a repackaging process and special advertising were all barriers that kept traditional companies out, but allowed an unknown like Midway to get started.

Starline added other handgun calibers and Midway offered them to the trade; then, three other important events occurred. First, Winchester, not wanting to be left out, began to offer bulk brass in 1984; our first order was for over a million dollars. Second, in 1986, the Firearms Owners Protection Act (Volkmer/McClure) became law; it amended the 1968 Gun Control Act to allow for the sale of ammunition and reloading components to 'individuals' across state lines. Third, last, and just before our tenth anniversary in 1987, Remington began offering bulk components and we became a distributor. No one could have predicted in 1980 the future impact that the original order of 357 Magnum brass would have on Midway, Starline and the reloading products and shooting sports industry. But today, it's quite clear.

Midway Arms, Inc. | 7450 Old Highway 40 West | Columbia, MO, 65203 | 18 June 1987

A dream come true for many reloaders in the early 1980s was a batch of fresh, shiny 357 Magnum brass, ready for loading.

The addition of a carbide steel insert, into the bottom of the resizing die, made reloading both the 38 Special and 357 Magnum a lot easier.

Early 357 Magnum ammunition was loaded with lead bullets, not modern jacketed hollow points.

This early S&W M-19 from 1956, with after-market Jordan-style grips, is chambered for 357 Magnum, but is much more comfortable to shoot with 38 Special ammo.

Computers
HOLY COW!

It would be difficult to overestimate the importance of computers in Midway's early years; when we opened in 1977, our cash register was the most complicated piece of electronic equipment in the gun shop. It had department keys and spit out a tape at the end of the day showing how much cash should be in the cash drawer; that was about it. Twenty-two years later we completed one last major step in the seemingly endless process of computerization.

Apparently it was all about being in the right place at the right time; as the Company grew and we needed to manage a growing list of Customers and products, along came IBM and Apple with powerful and affordable computers.

Computer workstations were only part of the solution. There was also software and a huge amount of personal and organizational learning. I'd taken a Fortran class (early computer programming language) in college and worked closely with the computer department during the first half of my Air Force tour; but I was soon to learn that neither of those experiences were of much value in computerizing the business.

In 1982 we bought our first computer, an Apple III with 128k of RAM, a stand-a-lone 5 megabyte hard drive and a daisywheel printer — for the grand sum of $10,000; then the learning began. Initially we only used it to type in Customer names and addresses, then print out labels for mailing our first flyers. It worked just fine for that limited need.

In early 1986 we upgraded to an IBM AT, with an internal 20 megabyte hard drive; and we chose a database software by Revelation. We were now beginning to get serious about computers and database management. By the end of the year we had figured out how to use it, entered all of our Customers and products, and began invoicing on January 2, 1987. By March we had two computers networked together. This was really an unbelievable system, for such a small company.

Photo by Erik Klein of vintage-computer.com.

Our first computer, an Apple III, back in 1982.

In the computer industry, technology was advancing very rapidly; the world was moving away from DOS and on to Windows, so we followed suit. Making this conversion was the biggest project we had ever attempted and it was two years of hard work before the job was complete; but we were a 'fully-computerized' small business and prepared for continued service to our Customers.

Midway Arms, Inc. | 5875 West Van Horn Tavern Road | Columbia, Missouri | October 1999

Photo by Erik Klein of vintage-computer.com.

Our second computer, an IBM AT, in 1986.

4-3/4" plastic disc that holds 4.7 gigabytes of data – unbelievable.

A current production 8 gigabyte removable thumb drive – unimaginable in 1982.

Computers

Cable

Printer

Computer networking is like Christmas tree lights wired parallel.

101

The $500,000 RIFLE

I kept one for myself, as a souvenir and to shoot. It is 54 caliber with brown steel furniture, serial #857PY01081 (made in 1982).

Luck is often described as being in the right place at the right time, with the 'special knowledge' and 'right tools' to take advantage of a situation — and an understanding of and willingness to take risk; certainly that's a good description of luck in this instance. It all started when the Browning representative walked into the gun shop, in February of 1983, to discuss the new Browning product offerings. He also advised that Browning was discontinuing the Jonathan Browning Mountain Rifle and had reduced the price considerably, from last year's $449.95 retail price.

The 'special knowledge' was being an owner and shooter of muzzle loading rifles and believing that shooters would want to buy this rifle in the spring and summer – allowing us to take advantage of generous early-payment discounts. The 'right tools' were having a Browning account, the gun shop to receive to and ship from and the experience to get advertisements in place right away.

Risk? There really wasn't much; an order of at least 16 guns would allow for fall dating - thus the discounts for early payment. We placed the first order, set the price at $295 each and sent ads to Shotgun News, Black Powder Times and Muzzleloader magazine — and waited. Then the phone started ringing – wow!

The rifles were available in 45, 50 and 54 caliber with either brass or brown steel furniture. Browning provided us with the quantity remaining for each model; the largest quantity being in 45 caliber, with brass furniture, and there were only about 150 of the 54 caliber guns with brown steel furniture.

Success often creates its own challenges; as soon as the demand was evident, we wanted to 'corner the market' — but only had a $10,000 line of credit. The representative suggested that we call the sales manager, not the credit manager, tell him our plan and ask for more credit. It worked; our credit limit was raised and we bought all the models that were in limited supply – paying for them as soon as they were sold. Then we asked for an even higher credit limit and bought all the remaining inventory.

In the course of just a few months, the little-known Midway Arms, Inc., in Columbia, MO sold over $500,000 worth of Jonathan Browning Mountain Rifles. It was just luck; we were in the right place at the right time . . .

At the Gun Shop | 7450 Old Highway 40 West | Columbia, MO | December 1983

A neat feature on the lock is the rams horn, surrounding the cleanout hole on the breech.

Percussion cap, powder, patch and ball – a cartridge without a case.

A modern buck skinner was featured on the instruction manual.

The possibles bag and powder horn carry everything needed for shooting and cleaning.

operation and care of the
**JONATHAN BROWNING
MOUNTAIN RIFLE** These instructions should be carefully noted.
VERY IMPORTANT–SAVE THIS BOOKLET

The History of
MidwayUSA
Part 3

My friend and college classmate Ralph Twellman (left) of Built-Rite Buildings, managed all of the additions to the original building on U.S. Highway 40.

It was an interesting year of transition – 1985, as we had just closed the gun shop. The phones rang, the mail came, we processed the orders and the little brown truck (UPS) took the packages away each day. It was a much easier business to run, but we missed the walk-in Customers. As the year began, our principle product was Starline handgun brass – ten different calibers, bearing the Midway name; but then our first shipment of Winchester rifle brass arrived in mid-January. We didn't have a loading dock, so we unloaded the truck by hand, one cardboard drum at a time, and carried them through the front door.

The Winchester deal was a game changer; imagine a small company, that didn't even have an account with Winchester until the previous July, being 'first-to-market' with Winchester bulk-packed rifle brass. It had never before been offered and our Customers loved it. Remington, not to be left out of this new market, began selling us bulk brass in 1987. Lee Precision was our first major reloading product line, also in 1987. Midway was running full-page ads in Shotgun News and was beginning to look a lot bigger than we actually were.

Harold Volkmer was our local U.S. Representative and James McClure was a U.S. Senator from Idaho. Together, with encouragement from the NRA, they sponsored what became known as the Volkmer/McClure act, passed in 1986.

This new law amended the 1968 Gun Control Act, allowing consumers to buy cartridge cases and bullets for reloading – by mail order, without the need for a Federal Firearms License. We also began to sell directly to the end user, and the orders really picked up.

Computerization of Order Processing was our first real step into the computer world. In January of 1987 we started processing our invoices via the computer and began networking multiple computers together in March. This was a giant, giant step.

We almost always had a building project going on – more space for storing inventory, taking orders and preparing shipments. In the end, our one acre lot was completely consumed by parking lot and the 10,000 sq. ft. building.

In December, 1988, our new 30,000 square foot building on Van Horn Tavern Road was completed, and we moved just over a mile to our new campus. Many important events had driven our growth, since closing the retail store just four years earlier.

7450 Old Highway 40 West | Columbia, MO | December 31, 1988

David Patterson, myself and Stan Frink, groundbreaking ceremony 1988.

This is the final configuration of our first building at 7450 Old Highway 40 West. The original 1,536 square feet had been expanded to 10,000 square feet. The original front door is under the awning.

The last addition to the building backed right up to our small garden.

(Left to Right) U. S. Representative Harold Volkmer from Missouri (1931 – 2011). and U.S. Senator James A. McClure from Idaho (1924-2011).

Credit: Missouri State Archives

Credit: U.S. Senate Historical Office

FAMILY
& FARM
the

This is the 'fun' section; there's nothing here that is terribly important, but it was fun to be part of these stories, fun to write them and I always smile when reading them. The Squirrel That Bit Me is a story from over 55 years ago, yet it's as vivid in my mind as if it happened yesterday. Though never intended, this story is reminiscent of something that Huckleberry Finn would have done a century earlier and twenty miles to the east, near the Mississippi River at Hannibal.

Stories like The Missouri Spring Trifecta are just my imagination running wild; there's a lot of time to think while waiting for the turkeys to 'engage' in the early morning. As the day progresses, with or without a bird, there's time to move around. More than once, I've harvested my turkey after semi-abandoning the turkey hunting and turning my attention to mushrooms and arrowheads.

Certainly one of my favorite memories of dad is Dad's Hula Popper and the Big Bass. There are so many lessons there, most of which we can all relate to.

The
SQUIRREL
that BIT ME

Innocent enough from a distance, but ferocious if you get too close.

Dad liked to hunt squirrels and regularly we would have fresh squirrel meat for lunch or supper, when I was growing up. There was a story he told us once about how he had pulled a wounded squirrel from a hollow tree by twisting a forked stick around its tail.

One summer my younger brother Jerry and I were exploring in the back pasture and walked through a small grove of walnut trees where we spooked a squirrel that was digging for walnuts. Interestingly, the squirrel didn't run up a tree; but rather, he ran into a small hole in the bottom of one.

We were just kids, so naturally we went over to check it out. The hollow part didn't go very far up the tree, as we could hear the squirrel chattering when we got close. Then I remembered dad's story about using a forked stick to pull a squirrel out of a hole like this. Of course, his squirrel was wounded; this one wasn't.

I was nine years old that summer, and was thought to be responsible enough to carry my own pocket knife; so we looked around and found a nice bush, from which I cut a forked stick about two feet long. It was easy enough to engage the squirrel with the stick; but boy was he mad. It was another thing entirely to get the forked part of the stick wrapped around his tail – since we were operating completely by feel. But then everything came together and I had the squirrel by the tail — and was pulling him out.

Now, the moral of this story is to 'always have a plan for the next step in the process' — which I didn't. The squirrel came out of the hole, but immediately turned his body, came up the stick and sunk his teeth into the skin around the knuckle of my left index finger. I got the message immediately and dropped the stick, at which time the squirrel's tail came undone and he scampered up the tree.

My pride was hurt a little, but not as much as my finger. Mom and dad were both sympathetic when I told the story, and of course I've told it to my kids and grandkids – showing them the scars — so they will be smart enough not to do something so 'innocent'.

Rural Marion County, Missouri | Summer of 1958

What are the chances of getting a forked stick wrapped around a squirrel's tail that you cannot see?

This is my best recollection of the forked stick.

This white oak closely resembles the walnut tree from my memory.

After all these years, the scars are still there; I can never forget.

The Best
PRAIRIE DOG
SHOOTING
Of My Life

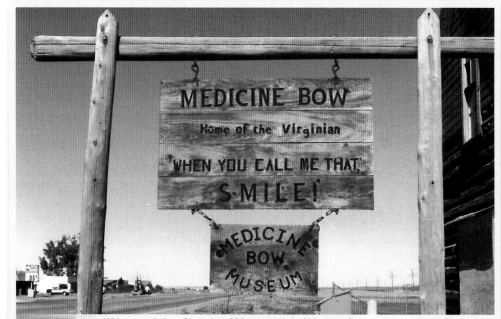

With a population of less than 300, some think of Medicine Bow as just a wide spot in the road.

"Just take the two-track to the right, under the power lines, and follow it till you get to **The Reservoir**; there are lots of prairie dogs there." Those were the words of the rancher, offering advice about the best prairie dog shooting on his ranch.

Medicine Bow, Wyoming was a hotspot for prairie dogs in the late 1980s. Gary Cole, from the old Petersen Publishing Company, stopped by just a few days before we were to leave for that year's planned prairie dog trip to South Dakota. He suggested I try Medicine Bow, as that's where Petersen entertained the outdoor writers. He told me where to stay, who to talk with and insisted there were tons of dogs. So, change of plan; we headed for Medicine Bow – thanks Gary!

The kids were both experienced enough to safely shoot .22s from the back of the pickup, so I rigged up a couple of swivel seats in the bed – with shooting rails and a sun roof. One of my buddies saw us come up over a ridge and began referring to my pickup as the "War Wagon" – a name that became my CB handle on prairie dog trips from then on.

Anyway, I was looking for **The Reservoir** and had followed the rancher's instructions but simply couldn't find it – hadn't gone far enough. After three or four miles and having driven completely out of prairie dogs, I stopped to glass out front. A long, long way out on the prairie was a tiny brown strip, with some ridges on it – it looked out of place in the green sagebrush. As I came to learn, this was the back side of the dam of **The Reservoir** and the ridges were cattle trails.

It was about 10:00 in the morning when we arrived and in my opinion, this area of the ranch had never been shot. The dogs were the thickest I have ever seen and apparently had never heard a gunshot — before now. We laid into them for a couple of hours then invited the rest of our group to follow us back to **The Reservoir** after our lunch break — for the last afternoon of shooting.

I made many more trips to Medicine Bow, after that, and never think or talk about prairie dog shooting without remembering **The Reservoir**. It was the very best!

Undisclosed ranch near Medicine Bow, Wyoming | June 1988

The Virginian Hotel was completed in 1911 and put on the National Register of Historic Places in 1978. Yes, you can still get a room there.

Sara and Russell were 12 and 14 that summer and were a bit spoiled with all the shooting. They're holding a small jackrabbit and their 10/22s.

What a great backdrop for a photo op. This is one of our annual prairie dog groups. (L-R) Sara Potterfield, Larry Potterfield, Jeff Larkin, Matt Fleming, Don Martin, Ryan Fischer, Dennis Holdmeier, Bob McNulty, Aaron Oelger, Stacey Uptegrove

Just a casual picture taken in late afternoon, standing in front of the Virginian Hotel.

MEDICINE BOW
Home of the Virginian
WHEN YOU CALL ME THAT
SMILE!

SARA'S FIRST BUCK

What a great confidence builder for an 11 year old girl to shoot such a nice deer. Of course her brother was jealous!

Hunting with an eleven year old daughter is an interesting experience. By that age she could sit quietly and pay attention for reasonable periods of time, so it was my job to present her with a deer that would stand still long enough for her to take a well-aimed shot.

Russell, her brother, had shot a doe from this same stand earlier that morning, so we were back, hoping for another one; it was 8:30 a.m. The stand was named "Grand Central Station" or "Grand Central" for short, because it is the confluence of three fields and three blocks of woods. There always seem to be deer moving through, which is how the stand got its name.

The 8-point buck trotted out of the woods on our right and into the field in front of us – about 50 yards away. We spotted him immediately and when he was directly in front of us, I whistled him to a stop. Sara eased into position and made a reasonably quick shot. The deer gave no indication he had been hit, but did a 180 and ran back into the woods he had come out of – and was still running when I lost sight of him.

We waited a few minutes for Sara and Russell to settle down, then climbed out of the stand and walked over to the spot at which the buck was last standing. There was no blood or hair – a 60 grain bullet from a 223 doesn't leave much of a blood trail. Sara decided that she must have missed and that we should just get back in the stand and wait for another one – but what does an eleven year old girl know?

I suggested we look in the woods where we last saw him. They were pretty open and as we entered I saw the white of his belly about 75 yards away. Sara again complained that we weren't going to find him and we should wait for another, but I suggested she look off to the left, while Russell and I looked to the right.

Well, Sara found her deer, all by herself, and was of course very excited. Twenty five years passed before she shot another deer that big.

Grand Central Deer Stand | Midway Farms | Columbia, MO | 14 November 1987

112

Big brother, Russell, shot this doe earlier that morning.

In 1987, the strategy was pretty much "anything with horns". This is a small five pointer and you're looking at the best side.

Russell and Sara on a Prairie Dog Trip in Wyoming.

We recovered the bullet — a 60 grain Hornady spire point. It's a bit light for serious deer hunting, but in this case it worked perfectly.

The Missouri SPRING TRIFECTA

The real prize, of course, is the gobbler. This one weighed 20-1/2 pounds, had a ten inch beard and one inch spurs. My Winchester Model 12 has taken lots of turkeys.

It may be quite a stretch, for some folks, as the word "Trifecta" is applied to spring turkey hunting in Missouri – especially for those who know horse racing; but for any hunter who's been fortunate enough to shoot a gobbler during Missouri's spring turkey season, then pick a batch of mushrooms, and finally to find an arrowhead – well, for them at least, using the word Trifecta may not seem such a stretch.

It was the twelfth day of the 21 day turkey season, but only my fourth morning in the woods; the NRA always seems to schedule their annual meetings during this time. In my previous three outings, I had hunted pretty passively, sitting by Raymond's food plot (named after Brenda's dad) and waiting for the turkeys to come to me – didn't work. Well, it kinda worked; the turkeys did come to the food plot, but not close enough to be of interest; and close is really important when you're turkey hunting.

This fourth morning was different; first I was hunting with a friend (Matt) and second, the plan was to go to the birds, to be more aggressive. We walked to the north end of the food plot (arriving about 5:45 a.m.), made an owl call and listened to several responses. The nearest bird was off the southwest corner of the food plot, about 500 yards away – so we walked back to the south end, then turned west into the woods. Crossing a small ditch, we set up near some cedar trees on the side of the hill. It was a classic hunt; we were only about 100 yards out, and the bird was still on the roost, Matt called him in and I made the shot. One and done at 6:12 a.m., pretty short turkey hunt!

The mushrooms were simply 'in the way' as we walked through the woods back to the pickup; no real effort, no real mushroom hunt. Sometimes it works that way.

Now, the arrowhead was a different story. Matt and I moved to a place called Patton Farm to try for his turkey. There was a small creek running through the southeast corner of this farm, only about two hundred yards long. Half-way up the creek, in a couple inches of water, was the arrowhead. Perhaps this morning Matt and I added new meaning to the word Trifecta.

Hunting with Matt Fleming, President of MidwayUSA | Hunters Creek Farm | Howard County, Missouri | 2 May 2014

These morel mushrooms are the crème de la crème, and spring turkey season is the right time to look for them in Missouri.

Technically this isn't an arrowhead, but certainly it's a tool used by Native Americans in their day-to-day living. The Swiss Army Knife is just there for comparison. It's 2-1/2 inches long.

Brenda is carefully walking a big log looking for mushrooms. She's got a bag full in one hand and her Winchester Model 12 in the other.

Part one of the Missouri Spring Trifecta.

40 YARD DASH
for a Turkey

It took a while for me to decide to tell this story, because I was running with a loaded gun; so hopefully everyone understands that as an experienced hunter, and someone who has participated in shooting competitions that require moving with a loaded gun, I felt perfectly safe. Please don't try this if you don't have the experience to do it safely.

Spring turkey hunting in Missouri can be frustrating; sometimes the gobblers go quiet and other times they gobble their heads off — hung up just out of range. This morning was the latter. I was positioned in the edge of a woods near the bottom of a long, narrow field that came to a point. The woods behind me was called 'Turkey Hollow' – and it's one of my favorite hunting spots.

A lone tom was with some hens on the other side of the field about 70 yards out; and I'd been working him for twenty minutes or so – but to no avail. The field was slightly higher in the middle, so that when down on my knees I couldn't see the turkeys and they couldn't see me. Standing up behind a tree, the top half of the birds were in sight and the gobbler was in full strut at the edge of the field, with a few hens. The rest of the hens were moving out through the woods; it was now or never, but I needed to get 40 yards closer!

After checking the safety on my Winchester Model 12, I took the position of a sprinter, ready to spring out of his blocks; then I gave a cluck. Knowing that it took a tom turkey a second or two to come out of strut, as soon as the next gobble hit my ears I made my dash, keeping low with shotgun in my right hand.

As I neared the top of the ridge, the first birds to fly were the hens; then, there was the gobbler – just coming out of strut. I kept going straight at him; he started to run downhill to my left and took flight. As soon as he got in the air, I straightened up, stopped and shot him from about 30 yards, just like you would shoot a clay pigeon. And that was the end of my 40 yard dash for a turkey.

Midway Farms | Fayette, Missouri | 5 May 2001

An Eastern Gobbler, up close and in full strut, is a magnificent sight.

This old Winchester Model 12 was made in 1938 and has been my favorite turkey gun for many years.

In the early years I guided Brenda, but soon she was turkey hunting on her own and guiding other hunters.

Vietnam-era jungle fatigues, given to me by a friend, were great for turkey hunting.

Larry at the Cabin, with Turkey and Model 12.

DEER CAMP

Three generations of the Potterfield family gather around the campfire at mid-day, during opening weekend.

Nothing quite excites or satisfies like the anticipation of opening morning of deer season; at best, the night before is restless. Sure the anticipation dulls a little with age, as dreams of the 30 point buck are replaced by the reality of what's been shot there over the last twenty years.

Deer camp is one of the most cherished traditions in the hunting community – and for good reason; it's a gathering place for multiple generations of family and friends, many of whom see each other only during that special time.

The young folks and newbies always liven things up. They provide new opportunities to talk about deer rifles and cartridges and of course gun safety — to retell and listen again to the worn-out stories of hunts gone by, often with important facts left out. They represent one more chance to teach how to judge the size and age of a buck and how to tell a button buck from a doe or female fawn — how to be quiet when walking through the leaves and how to climb in and out of a deer stand.

First light is always magic; shapes and movement in the imagination turn into something or nothing as the binoculars come into focus. With each passing

moment, everything brightens up and soon the day is full on. The woods are much quieter in the fall than during spring turkey season; sure the crows and geese are still around, but mating season for the song birds is over – and the turkeys hardly ever gobble. Perhaps there's some wind in the trees and hopefully the serious rustling of leaves, as Mr. Majestic makes his way past the stand.

Mid-day at deer camp is a chance to warm up and chow down; perhaps get a nap and lament that it's unseasonably warm or cold or wet or dry. That's when I like to hang around outside, sitting on a stump and tending a roaring campfire, with grandkids chasing each other and playing in the leaves. There aren't enough moments like that in a lifetime.

And yes, there are the deer stories, one person saw nothing but does, another missed a big buck. The wind was right, the wind was wrong. "I'll need some help tracking this one." Deer camp will always have a very special place on my calendar and in my heart.

Deer Camp | Midway Farms | Fayette, Missouri | 26 November 2014

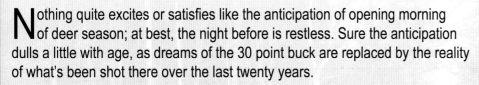

Chris Cauley, with his best whitetail – to date; 160 class bucks, like this, are on the far side of the Bell curve — in this part of Missouri.

When the weather is cold or rainy, an enclosed blind — on a stand or the ground – allows for longer, more comfortable time in the field. The food plot has beans, wheat and turnips.

Seven and nine year olds, Jay and Eliza, lead mom to the cabin for morning brunch.

For grandkids of this age, a fun part of deer camp is playing in the leaves at mid-day – (L-R) Jay, Benjamin, Nathaniel and Oliver.

The
DRIVEN
PARTRIDGE
Shoot

Sara and I pose in traditional English garb, just after a drive. The shotguns are the pair of Holland and Hollands that Sara used on this trip.

A driven bird shoot had been on my wish list for years, but when the invitation came, I almost didn't go. After looking at the price tag, my answer was "no"; but Brenda suggested that it would be a great opportunity for me to spend some quality time with our daughter – OK, I'll go.

Naturally, I had a lot of ideas about how a driven bird shoot worked; but the experience was far grander than I was expecting. The European tradition of driven bird shooting, the other guests (including two from Holland & Holland), the food and the castle - which dates back to the 16th century - provided an unbelievable backdrop for the main event – shooting driven birds – red legged partridge.

For me the most interesting part was the shotguns, the actual shooting and the bird drives – twelve in total, over three days. The best reason to own a matched-pair of fine English side by side shotguns is to shoot driven birds – that is, to use them for their intended purpose. Sara took Holland and Hollands and I took Purdeys – both 12 bore; but most of the other shooters used 20 gauge over/under guns, and one guest shot a pair of 28 gauges.

The shooting was mostly incoming birds, with a few crossers – all birds were in range and at times I had too much choke. On some drives we had a couple seconds to shoot, after acquiring a target; but on other drives we held our guns at the ready and shot before you could say one thousand and one. Sitting on our right side, facing to the rear, was our loader. We handed off our empty (and still closed) shotgun with our right hand, extending the left hand to the front; immediately the warm barrels of the loaded gun found our palms. When the sky was full of birds, it was a shot a second.

Now, they've been shooting driven partridge on this ranch for 150 years, because its plateaus and canyons are ideally suited for such. There were 45 drivers on foot in each drive, pushing the partridges until they flew off the plateau, over the canyon to the plateau on the other side. Yes, we eleven shooters were lined up, one per peg, in the bottom of the canyons, about 50 yards apart. At the end of each drive, all I could say was **wow!**

Ventosilla Castle | 20 minutes south of Toledo, Spain | 20 October 2014

My guns were a matched pair of Purdeys, shown here with a brace of partridge.

This drive is over; from the number of shells left in the ammo holder, this was a light shooting peg.

The shooting party, with guests, in front of Ventosilla Castle — with a day's shoot of partridge in the foreground. Sara and I are on the far right; the Holland and Holland folks on the far left. Photo courtesy Guy Davies, Holland and Holland, New York.

There's a lot of hunting tradition in this old castle, lots of red stags and wild boars and a few African trophies.

DAD'S GUNS

Dad's favorite rifle was a Remington Model 12, made in October, 1935. I inherited it upon his death. (Note the Fajen stock I installed has a pistol grip.)

Gilbert was his given name, but everyone called him Bert; and he was a pretty good hunter and trapper. For dad, a gun was simply a tool he needed to hunt for food or fur and to run his trap line. In my early years, he only had three guns — a shotgun and two .22 rifles.

His shotgun was an old 12 gauge Belgian-made side by side, with outside hammers and twist steel barrels; the metal and wood finish were well-worn and the action was loose — the kind of gun you aren't supposed to shoot. But shoot it he did; and he brought home lots of quail, ducks and geese. When I got older and 'smart enough' to know that his old shotgun was dangerous, I sold it for him (a hundred bucks) and he put the money toward a modern Remington 870 pump – that he never could remember to shuck.

The first of his .22 rifles was a Stevens Crackshot that he used for killing hogs when they were butchering. It was pretty much worn out and dad kept it in an old brooder house that he was using for his beekeeping supplies. One summer day, when Cousin Charlie was visiting from St. Louis and dad was at work, I or my younger brother snuck in through one of the lower house doors and got the gun. We shot frogs in a pond behind the house and of course mom heard the shots and told dad.

I don't remember anyone getting a whipping, but when dad heard the story, he broke the gun in half and threw it in the pond.

He had owned the other .22 for many years – a Remington Model 12 pump action repeater. Dad was born in 1910 and this rifle was made in 1935; likely he bought it from a local hardware store, as that was where you bought guns in those days.

Growing up in the country, I shot thousands of rounds through that rifle at rabbits, squirrels, raccoons, opossums, frogs, birds, snakes and tin cans. Dad had dropped it out of a tree once and broke the stock, which he had taped up with electricians tape. During high school shop class, in my freshman year, I made a new stock for it; but a so-so job, so I replaced it with one made by Fajen a few years later.

Mom passed the gun on to me after dad's death, in 1989.

Ely, Missouri | 4 April 1989

Dad's gun, at the top, has no original finish and please notice the wear to the bottom of the forend. Bottom gun has original factory finish.

Dad bought a used Marlin 30-30 in the 1960s. Here he is with a doe he apparently shot in the head.

The Remington Rocket .22 short ammunition was introduced in 1956. There were 28 cartridges to the pack and they cost about a penny each. I shot lots of this ammo.

Winter 1947 picture of Dad with my older brother Marion, and a pretty good bunch of rabbits. That's dad's Remington Model 12 hanging above them.

The lower gun is what dad's would have looked like when he bought it 1935 or 36; dad's gun above, after a lifetime of serious use.

Remington "ROCKET" 22 SHORT
MADE IN U.S.A.
NON-CORROSIVE KLEANBORE PRIMING

FIRST RIFLES for the KIDS

The top rifle is Russell's; it's a Winchester Model 67, Sara's below is a Remington 514.

On their respective fourth birthdays, each of our two children received his/her first rifle and got to shoot it. Now at four years of age, they didn't get to keep these rifles in their rooms; we kept them in the vault and brought them out regularly during the spring, summer and fall - so they could continue to enjoy their fourth birthday presents — and learn how to safely handle and shoot them. Looking back, my recommendation to parents today might be that they wait till the kids are six or seven — and take lots of pictures.

Back in the late 1970s, no gun company made a .22 rifle small enough for a four year old, so I bought an older single shot .22 rifle and spent a few evenings after work converting it for the intended use. Russell's rifle is a Winchester Model 67 youth model. It was made in the early 1960s and someone had poorly cut a hole and fit a Kennedy half-dollar into the right side of the stock. As it was no longer of interest to gun collectors, I got a pretty good deal. Being a youth model, it had a 20" barrel – which was fine; I just had to shorten the forend and reshape it, then shorten the butt and re-fit the buttplate. Thinning and sanding the stock eliminated the half-dollar pocket and 30 coats of Tru-Oil finished it off.

When Sara turned four, she was a bit smaller than Russell had been at that age. In my mind, she needed a lighter rifle and one that cocked on closing rather than by pulling back the hammer – as on Russell's Model 67. The Remington Model 514 was the answer. This was also a 1960s production gun, with the straight (non-tapered) barrel, making it a bit lighter. I had the barrel shortened to 16-1/4" and the front sight reset; then I shortened, reshaped and refinished the stock as on Russell's gun, two years before.

Our former four year olds now have children of their own, and they still have the presents they received on their fourth birthday. Of course, the grandchildren are all learning to shoot with these .22 rifles made by Remington and Winchester in the 1960s and re-purposed by loving hands in the 1970s. Though we couldn't fully appreciate it at the time, these were gifts that truly have kept on giving.

MidwayUSA | Columbia, Missouri | 7 October 2014

Russell and Sara, in the turkey woods, with a Winchester Model 12, 20 gauge - Spring 1988.

Russell (age 12, with a Remington 870 20 gauge youth model) had been wing shooting for a couple of years and Sara (age 10, with a Winchester Model 37 youth model) was just getting started in 1986.

Pure entertainment; what great fun to watch kids or grandkids break balloons with a .22 rimfire. A golf tee, between the lip and the knot, holds the balloon firmly to the ground.

Today parents can buy kids their first rifles right off the shelf, like this Crickett Rifle by Keystone Sporting Arms.

HORNETS, WASPS & BEES
Oh My!

Yellow Jacket

Bumble Bee

Honey Bee

Bald Faced Hornet

It was lunchtime in the African bush and three of us were sitting at a table under a shade tree. November is the dry season and often a curious honey bee will cruise around the lunch table looking for anything wet. We were engaged in conversation when I took a swig of beer. Immediately it was clear that there was something in my mouth besides beer; I spit it out, but not before the bee got his stinger into my upper lip – wow!

Another time in Africa, I was following Brenda and the rest of the team on an elephant track; it led us across a large open area and past a small tree. The PH and trackers all stepped around the tree, as the limbs were hanging pretty low; but Brenda simply stooped a bit and walked under it. Immediately she began screaming, swatting her head with her hands and running; there was a wasp nest in that tree. She was lucky to have received only one sting – on the face.

Back home, in the summer of 1985, I was leading my brother in law Bill, his son Chris and my son Russell into the squirrel woods. Russell was in the rear and our two guests were in the middle, when all hell broke loose. We had walked over a nest of yellow jackets and all ran like crazy out of the woods, with Bill and Chris pulling off their shirts and swatting at their attackers. Russell and I somehow escaped the wrath of the yellow jackets, but our guests were both stung multiple times. Needless to say, the squirrel hunting was over.

I remember a Potterfield family picnic, back when I was just a kid; cousin Johnny had to visit the outhouse and no one knew there was a bumble bee nest inside. Johnny was either the first one to use the outhouse, or somehow disturbed them. He received several bumble bee stings before he could make his exit.

The bald-faced hornets build large gray nests, mostly on tree limbs. I've never personally had a run-in with these folks, probably because they are hanging a bit higher in the trees; but each fall, during deer season, I look for them and am reminded that anyone who spends much time outside during the warmer months is going to have encounters with hornets, wasps and bees. The good news is that you won't see it coming!

Midway Farms | Fayette, Missouri | 18 November 2014

They look pretty good hanging in your office, but make sure they are empty first.

Lunch in the African Bush, Fred Blochet (PH) on the right and Bert Klineburger in the middle. (Nov 2007)

The bald-faced hornet nest. Birds have begun to tear it apart, exposing the inner workings.

As long as you don't get much closer to bees than this, they normally aren't a problem.

A
November to
Remember

W e named it 'Grand Central Station' back in 1985 — 'Grand Central' for short — when we first hunted there. In the fall the deer often move through this area all day long, as there are large tracts of woods on the east, the west and the north — with the necks of the crop fields all coming together in an old fencerow. Through the years we've added a food plot and a heated blind, allowing us to comfortably hunt in the rain or the cold.

This story actually begins back in 1987; Russell, Sara and I were sitting on a makeshift platform in the old fencerow. Russell had shot a doe earlier and it was now Sara's turn to shoot. A nice 8-pointer came out from the right, crossing about 50 yards in front of us. I whistled the buck to a stop and Sara plugged him – she was eleven years old.

Fast forward twenty-seven years; Sara is the guide and her daughter Eliza and son Jay are the hunters. Last year the kids had shot their first does, and this year they were allowed to hunt bucks. Jay's opportunity came the second morning of the early youth season; the buck came out of the woods at the end of the food plot and walked across the field to a salt lick – on the west side. 125 yards is quite a distance for a seven year old to shoot. Sara grunted him to a stop seven times as he crossed the field, but Jay could never quite get comfortable and didn't shoot. The deer went into the woods and Jay cried, because he really wanted that buck. Twelve minutes later, out came the same deer, but this time at only 40 yards – and Jay's aim was true.

Two weeks later, it was opening day of the rifle season and mother and daughter were back in the blind at 'Grand Central'. Now it was Eliza's turn. Her

Mom (Sara) with nine year old daughter Eliza and her first buck.

buck came into the food plot from the right, about 60 yards out. She quickly put on her glasses and earmuffs, then took careful aim and made the shot.

Two nice bucks, taken in the same area that mom took her first one twenty-seven years earlier, might just start a tradition and certainly made it a November to Remember.

Grand Central Station | Midway Farms | Fayette, Missouri | 2nd and 15th of November 2014

First buck for mom – twenty-seven years ago.

Eliza, looking for deer in the woods.

First buck for seven year old Jay.

Jay doesn't know how to use it yet, but he's getting an early orientation.

My
FAVORITE
SHOTGUN
for Turkeys

An Eastern tom turkey is always a great trophy; it's even more special with a favorite shotgun (1990 photo).

In my opinion, the most exciting thing about springtime in Missouri is turkey season; sure there are mushrooms to pick in the woods, fish to catch in the ponds and rivers, and arrowheads to find in the ditches — but nothing quite compares with being in the woods with our big Eastern tom turkeys during the mating season in April and May. For me, it's a time to hunt, as well as an opportunity to get some exercise and spend time with family and friends.

The hunting is never the same from one day to the next; I've used box calls, mouth calls and sometimes no call at all. I've hunted from ground blinds and deer stands, but mostly just on foot. I've called them in, chased them down, ambushed them and headed them off at the pass. I've shot them on the ground, in the air and on tree limbs — every legal way you can shoot a turkey, I've done it. I've hunted in the rain, in the snow and on some of the most beautiful and pleasant spring mornings on earth.

Some days it's only me, getting into the woods just after 5:00 a.m. and waking up the gobblers; then going in tight and hoping luck is on my side. But most of the time family and friends are involved; and that just makes it more special. As the mornings go on, it's true hunting, moving and calling, then moving and calling again, and again; till the morning is gone or my time or energy runs out.

Now turkey hunting wouldn't be the same without my favorite shotgun – for hunting turkeys. You've heard the old adage: "Beware the man with one gun, he may know how to use it." Let me assure you I've never supported that idea, and like a different gun for almost every occasion.

My favorite shotgun for turkeys is an old Winchester Model 12, 12 gauge, made in 1940. Half of the original finish has been worn off this old gun, but it has a nice bore and a 30" full choke, solid rib barrel. It's balanced well, has a good trigger pull, patterns like a swarm of honey bees and hits right where you point it. Yes, I have missed a couple of turkeys – by pulling the shot, but this old Model 12 has never let me down.

Hunter's Creek Farm | Howard County, Missouri | 2 May 2014

Old shotguns, with modern steel barrels, are almost always better with modern ammunition.

Daughter Sara also shoots a Model 12 for turkeys.

Russell's first turkey, and he used a Winchester Model 12.

Different clothes and a few more years of experience – but same, favorite turkey gun (2014 photo).

DAD was a BEEKEEPER

My dad Gilbert, in 1988, with his three remaining beehives. This is a spring picture and dad has added a honey production super to the far hive body.

Sometimes it's the little things that stick in your mind; Dad was a beekeeper. It wasn't a major part of his life, just a hobby really. The most colonies I ever remember him having was 25. But the bees were always there, while I was growing up, and the images and inner workings are still keen in my mind.

Beekeeping is very process oriented; you have to take care of bees year-round, add supers during the honey production cycles, harvest the surplus honey at the right time, clean it up and then sell it. Serious beekeeping is a much bigger job than most folks would imagine.

A bee colony has two missions – to make honey (as food for the colony) and to make more bees. In the late spring, if bee production has been good, the queen bee and half or so of the workers leave the hive to start a new colony. Upon departing, they gather on some nearby object – often a tree limb, and wait for the scouts to return and lead them to their new home. One of the jobs my brother Jerry and I got paid for was capturing the escaping swarms by puffing smoke on them (to calm them down), then cutting off the limb and laying the swarm in front of a newly prepared bee hive. The bees moved right in; Dad got a new swarm and Jerry and I split 50 cents for our efforts.

Periodically dad would check the progress of the honey production; then early summer and late fall he would harvest the honey, by removing most of the honey-laden supers from the hive bodies.

Preparing the honey for market was next. Comb honey boxes were inspected, scraped of extra beeswax, and boxed. For liquid honey, the wax caps of the honey cells were sliced off; then the honey was spun out using a large crank-type centrifuge, in the well-heated old brooder house. Finally the honey had to be screened, bottled and labeled.

After all that, the honey was ready to be sold – to neighbors or the local grocery stores. At first I went along with dad, but as a teenager, I made a few sales calls on my own. Dad's beekeeping activities were a small thing, in the big picture of life, but the hard work and attention to detail made a lasting impression on me.

Ely, Missouri | 4 April, 1989

Swarms of bees departing the hive will attach to almost anything. Mostly I remember them on the low-hanging limbs of the box elder trees over the hives.

The tools of the trade — simple but functional. The pry bars were broken leaf springs from an old car or buggy. Smoke from the smoker calmed the bees down.

This is dad, posing in front of his pickup, with a couple of boxes of comb honey.

The
Arrowhead
HUNTER

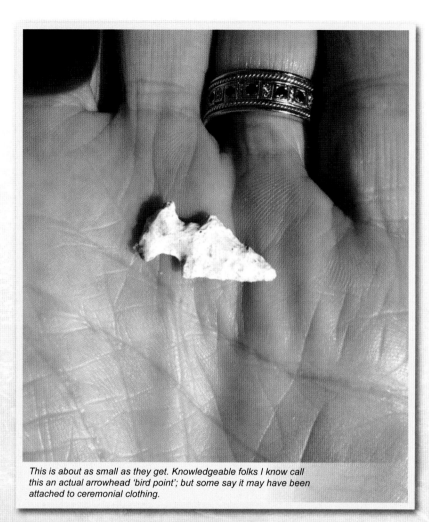

This is about as small as they get. Knowledgeable folks I know call this an actual arrowhead 'bird point'; but some say it may have been attached to ceremonial clothing.

Dad collected arrowheads and he had a cigar box full of his best ones. I don't recall that he actually took the time to hunt for them, but likely walked upon them while hunting, fishing or running his trap line — and simply picked them up.

It's a little different for me, I actually like to walk the tilled fields and the ditches and creeks looking for them – especially just after a serious rain. Brenda often accompanies me on these outings and that is her hand holding the bird point above – which she found. You might say that we find it relaxing, although the tilled fields can be tough walking if you get into them too soon after a rain; and some of the creeks would be good obstacle courses.

"Rocks" are what some of us call them and when showing off a new "rock" at work, someone always says "I've never found one, what do you look for?" The answer is simple, but complicated; you don't have to look for a completely exposed, flat on the ground, dirt-free 'rock' – those will almost always find you, because even small ones are easy to see. What you are looking for is a small part of a 'rock' wherein the edge has been carefully chipped to form serrations (as in the accompanying pictures); the rock may be mostly buried in the dirt or covered with leaves, and you will see only the tip, corner or edge. Color varies, so don't just look at white rocks, and be sure and go very, very slow and look carefully.

Another frequent question is "How old is it?" For this I defer to archaeologists who say they vary from 1,000 to 12,000 years.

Some people find more arrowheads than others and that is mostly due to time in the field, and location. My favorite story about arrowheads occurred several years ago when I found my first small bird point. I showed it off to Stan Frink, a friend at work, commenting that Dad only had one this small in his collection and this was my first small one; "had he ever found one this small?", I asked. His short reply was "yep, have a whole pill bottle full of em; used to run the back furrow behind the plow, when I was a kid and Dad was plowing the bottoms up home."

Perche Creek Watershed | Boone County | Columbia, Missouri | 4 November 2014

When sending a picture of this axe head to my son, I told him it probably wasn't worth a hundred dollar bill, but it sure looked good lying beside one.

After we accumulate 25-30 rocks, we like to take them out of the cigar box and mount them for display.

A hat or keys or pocket knife, provides perspective as to size. It's easy to spot them when they are completely exposed.

I like to take a picture of each rock, just as I found it; this knife blade was in a creek bed under a couple inches of running water.

DAD'S Hula Popper and the BIG BASS

This old Bronson 1500 Meteor bait casting reel (back) is similar to the one Dad had used for years, before mom gave him a new-fangled Johnson spin-cast outfit.

Dad was a reasonably serious fisherman, from my perspective – mostly for food, not sport. In our area of Missouri many of the larger ponds and lakes were stocked with largemouth bass, bluegill and channel cat. I have vague memories of some of the stories Dad told about big fish he had caught, either with hook and line or his bare hands; but this is a story I tell about him.

His only fishing rod was an old bait casting outfit, with 40# test braided line that would haul in just about anything, including big snapping turtles and tree limbs. Dad's strategy was to 'horse them in', once the hook was set; and with the 40# test line, he could do just that.

One year Mom gave him a Johnson's spin-cast reel for Father's Day. This new outfit had lightweight monofilament line (6 or 10# test), with an adjustable drag; and would throw a small artificial lure (like a Hula Popper) clear across a small pond. In the summer, Dad worked six days a week at a rock quarry; but summer days were long and sometimes my brother Jerry and I talked Dad into taking us fishing after work. There was a nice five acre

lake just a half mile north of home and we could be in the jon boat just five minutes after leaving the house. Dad had his new Johnson fishing outfit, but we boys just had willow poles and fishing worms.

On the south side of the lake, Dad hooked a very big bass. He had rowed the boat into position, cast his Hula Popper just outside the weeds and began popping it as he reeled it in. The big bass slammed it and dad commenced to pull; unfortunately he hadn't learned how to use lightweight monofilament line and a drag — so the big bass broke his line in just a few seconds.

The next day, Jerry and I were walking the water's edge and found the Hula Popper – as the bass had shook it clear. We proudly presented it to Dad that evening and begged him to have another try at the big bass. It was déjà vu; same place, same bass, same Hula Popper, same broken line. Dad hooked and lost that fish three times, before it got smart or developed a sore mouth.

The Big Lake | Potterfield Family Farm | Marion County, Missouri | Summer, 1962

The Hula Popper floats and after the bass shook it out of his mouth, the wind would drift it to the edge of the lake.

Bass, bluegill and channel catfish were stocked in many Missouri lakes and ponds.

This isn't the actual fish, because Dad never got it in the boat; this one's probably a bit larger than the one that got away — 9 pounds 14 ounces, taken from Falcon Lake, Texas in 1985.

Dad, in his later years, hauls a small bass out on the grass.

GUIDING the GUIDES

Beautiful bird; notice the thickness of the brush.

Brenda has a great passion for turkey hunting – far greater than mine — and it was she that came up with the idea of hunting the Ocellated Turkey, that lives mostly down in the area of the Yucatan Peninsula of old Mexico. For her it was part of a collection of turkeys she wanted to complete, for me it was just the love of hunting – new places, new game, new people and new customs.

It's interesting to think how the Mayan people must have related to this turkey, during the time they were building what we now call the Mayan ruins – some of which we visited after the hunt; they were only a short drive away. The jungle is very thick there and likely there are some ruins deep in the brush that have not yet been discovered.

These turkeys don't compare with the Eastern Turkey that we hunt in Missouri. They're quite a bit smaller and don't gobble or come to a call. Also, they look like first cousins to a peacock, and are stunningly beautiful, when mounted in a strutting pose.

Hunting was from makeshift blinds, over shelled corn thrown out on the roads and trails — or near water holes in the afternoon, where the birds came to drink. Everything was routine, except for Brenda's second turkey. We were set up a few hundred yards apart, watching separate water holes, when I heard her shoot. As it was about time to quit for the day and her waterhole was on the way out, we pulled up and walked on over to hear the story.

She had taken the shot across a water hole and the turkey flew off. The guides were just going to go after another bird, when I suggested that we take a look for feathers where the bird was standing. We saw some evidence that it had been hit at which time the guides pointed in the direction the bird had flown; so we lined up in pheasant drive formation and proceeded forward. We flushed him about 100 yards out, and I got off the only shot, missing him as he flew back in the direction from which we had just come, with one leg dangling. We did an about face and this time Brenda spotted him on the ground and shot him before he took to the air. Sometimes you have to 'guide the guides'.

Campechi, Mexico | 18 April 2011

138

Back at camp, I marvel at the beautiful colors.

This was Brenda's first gobbler. These ruins are modern, not Mayan.

Mostly it was trails through the jungle, not roads, and travel was by four-wheeler, and then on foot.

Three happy hunters, with morning gobblers; (L-R) Brent Lawrence of NWTF, myself and Brenda.

DEER & BIG GAME HUNTING

Whitetail deer hunting came much later in life for me than for my kids and grandkids. You see, there simply weren't many deer in northern Missouri when I was growing up. One summer, when I was eight or ten, I remember going with Dad to see the Missouri Department of Conservation turn loose a small trailer load of deer on a place we called the Goat Ranch, a mile or so northwest of Ely. It was many years after that before I shot my first whitetail in Missouri.

Perhaps as a result of that late start on deer, big game hunting also came later in life; but it might also be that for the first several years after starting the business, there wasn't enough time or money to support it.

It was actually some of the stories in this section that got the Short Stories project started in the first place. I had written a few of them, although not in the current format, and we decided to standardize the word count and add pictures so they could be published on Facebook and the MidwayUSA website. Everything has a beginning!

The WORLD'S SHORTEST
Grizzly Bear Hunt

Just having a little fun with this picture; Castle Peak in the background.

In the time it takes you to read this story, the grizzly bear hunt started and ended – about 60 seconds. I thought about titling this story "From bare to bear in 60 seconds".

Brenda and I were half-awake, but still snug in our sleeping bags, when we heard footsteps rapidly approaching our tent. The words from our guide were quickly, but softly-spoken - and very distinct: "Get-up quickly, bring your guns, a bear just chased me across the creek!"

We bailed from our sleeping bags and into our clothes. "Hurry folks, he is just behind the cabin and I am afraid the boys will have to shoot him!" We quick-tied our shoes, grabbed our guns and stepped out of the tent.

"Now folks, please chamber a round very quietly; any metallic sound may scare him away!"

We took three quiet steps toward the cabin. "There he is Larry, just to the right of that pole, shoot him!" In one of those rare moments when guide and hunter see the same thing at the same time, my eyes locked on those of the bear, facing us at 59 steps. I shifted a little to the right to clear some brush, then raising my 300 Win Mag and holding just under his chin, I fired. The Nosler 165 grain Partition did its job. He turned, ran 70 yards and collapsed.

Now, here's the rest of the story; and it doesn't count toward the 60 seconds.

The evening before, we had packed a moose in from spike camp – off to the west. In checking our trail, we discovered that this bear had followed that trail into camp, likely from the smell of moose on the packs. He apparently arrived just before daylight, as he had eaten only a little of our moose meat.

At about 6:20 a.m. that morning our guide had checked on a horse, picketed a short distance from the cabin. In returning, he encountered the bear and made his dash to our tent. Those were the footsteps that started the story.

Just south of Castle Peak | Wrangell Mountains of Alaska | 26 August 2004

The cabin at our Castle Peak camp.

This interior grizzly will square about 7-1/2 feet. My rifle is a custom, lightweight Remington 700 in 300 Win Mag.

It was late afternoon when the guides arrived from the moose camp to the west. The bear apparently followed the scent of the moose meat right into our camp.

The
BEAR
that Killed a
BEAR

Here is an unusual picture that provides a good perspective of the size of a coastal brown bear. To size the bear (how big he was), we measure the extreme length and width of the hide (after skinning), then average the two. This bear is 10' 0".

We saw him just at last light, way off to the south, as he lumbered down out of the willows toward the lakeshore – wow, was he big!

Next morning we climbed a steep hill on the opposite side of the lake, which gave us a great perspective of that entire area from about 1200 to 1500 yards distance. It was a beautiful, but hazy, October day and we saw several bears come and go around the lake. Early in the afternoon a large sow and two cubs walked down the far shoreline and a big bear suddenly came out of the bushes and chased them away – it was our bear.

We quickly descended from our perch and crossed the lake in a small boat, landing a half-mile down the shore, for the best wind. Our stalk was inland at first, aiming to cut off his escape to the willows at the base of the mountain, should he sense us.

Then we turned back toward the shore and my guide put me up front as we got near. I led quietly onward, through intermittent waist-high brush, with my 375 H&H at the ready. The bear was lying out of sight on a large mound of sod, but at 60 yards he sensed our presence and raised up on all four legs, giving me a two second broadside opportunity. One 300 grain Nosler Partition in the shoulder as he started to move, and another as he tumbled around on the ground, and the first part of this story was over – but wait, there is more!

Walking up on the kill site we found that our bear had stripped most of the sod in a circle nearly 50 feet in diameter and formed the mound he was standing on when I shot – interesting! We presumed he had killed a moose the night before.

While the guides were skinning the bear, Brenda got a shovel and started digging in the mound of sod. Oh my gosh; the bear had killed another bear, and not a small one either. We dug out both front feet and the head to get an idea of his size, but then left him to nature.

So, that's the story of the bear that killed a bear.

Port Moller | On the Alaska Peninsula | 4 October 2009

The bear, just as we first saw him, after the shots. Notice how he had stripped the sod from all around, to cover up the other bear.

Brenda taking a break from digging out the other bear.

Our bear hunts over, we still had two days left in base camp. These are silver salmon – sometimes a bonus to fall bear hunters.

The bear that was killed by the other bear. This is as far as we dug him out.

SLIDING for SHEEP

Larry and Brenda high in sheep country.

"**C**an we get closer?" Those were my words to the guide, as we looked down the mountain at the seven rams – nearly 600 yards away.

We had been working these rams for four days, but bad luck with fog, horses and terrain had been our lot. Now we were a mere 600 yards above them, on the same hillside, watching them feed along in a line from left to right. But 600 yards is twice as far as I like to shoot.

From our camp, at the bottom of the valley, the grassy hillside looked pretty smooth; but when you are actually sitting on such a hillside, things are quite different. The ground rises and falls in such a fashion that all seven rams had soon fed out of sight.

"Let's get closer!", I said. With rifles in one hand and backpacks in the other, down the mountain our small group went – with only our bottoms and the heels of our boots making contact with the ground – we were sliding to the sheep.

The grade was like one to one, which meant for every foot we went forward, we descended one foot, and we were going straight down, not side-hilling. In a hundred and fifty yards of 'free-sliding' we never saw the sheep, but stopped to look over a rise – still no sheep. "Let's get closer!", and away we went again.

Certainly they must have heard us, but when we stopped again for a look, still no sheep in sight – "We go again!"

Now, our guide carefully peeks over the rise then turns and says "Brenda, your sheep is in the front and Larry yours is third from the back." Of course when Brenda and I are hunting together, I always insist that she take the first shot. Sliding our backpacks in front of us to the top of the ridge, the sheep we had been looking at from 600 yards were now only 80 yards away.

Brenda shot first and her sheep went down. The rest of the rams started trotting away and I was preparing to take the second ram on the move, but he stopped after about 50 yards, as they almost always do, and I made it 'sheep for two'.

Wrangell Mountains of Alaska | August 2004

This is sheep country. Our sheep were in the area that is circled.

Base Camp – a large gravel bar island, with glacier water streams on both sides.

Beautiful, stunning, amazing, unbelievable – you choose the words.

Two nice Dall rams.

DEER & COYOTE
a Texas Pair

When deciding to shoot the coyote, it never occurred to me that the buck would hold, but he was with a doe that was bedded nearby – and never moved.

The Nail Ranch has lots and lots of whitetail deer – and a fair number of coyotes. In my many hunts there I have almost always got my buck and sometimes shot a doe or two for herd management; and every trip or two I get a coyote. In the early days, this was a true western hunt; we had a tented camp in a far off pasture called northwest Collins. Each morning we saddled up our horses, grabbed our Winchester saddle ring carbines and headed out to hunt. Besides the hunting and camp camaraderie, the very best part was the chuck wagon with an award-winning cook. He prepared three wonderful squares each day and told us stories around the campfire after dinner.

Time changes everything, they say; the old cook retired, the horses were replaced with pickup trucks, and we gave up the tented camp for the bunk house. It's still a wonderful hunting experience, but certainly not like the old days. For me personally, I haven't given up the tradition of the old guns and always take a period Winchester, Remington or Sharps rifle from the 19th or early 20th century.

This ranch is a great place to rattle for bucks during the rut, as the buck to doe ratio is quite high. A routine morning or afternoon is to drive around in the pickup, stopping at every canyon or mesquite flat where the wind is right and see what we can rattle up. Most of the deer we shoot there come in to the rattle.

However this particular afternoon we were looking over the flats and spotted this nice buck a ways off, and began the stalk. We were moving slowly through the scattered mesquite trees and had gotten undetected to within 125 yards – my self-imposed maximum for the open-sighted carbine. Then all of a sudden a coyote came into view from the right side at about 80 yards.

The guide said "that's a pretty-nice buck"; my response was that there were lots of nice bucks on the Nail and the coyote would be first. Maybe we would still have a chance at the buck. The coyote fell from a single shot and the buck didn't move an inch, so I levered another round into my Winchester and fired again. One coyote and one deer – about five seconds apart.

The Nail Ranch | Shackelford County | Albany, Texas | 13 November 1997

"That's a pretty-nice buck," said the guide, and he was quite surprised when I blasted the coyote first.

On warm fall days, the rattlesnakes are still out when deer season opens.

My rifle was a Winchester 1886 lightweight takedown in 45-70. It was made in 1914.

My good friend Roger Roberts also couldn't believe I shot the coyote first.

The ELK
I Didn't Shoot

I certainly wouldn't want to drink that water, would you?

"Did you shoot that big elk above the fireplace?" No, but I can tell you an interesting story about it!

We arrived in our New Mexico elk camp a day early, to allow for some scouting. The head guide said that he had flown over the area a few days earlier and there were elk everywhere. They even saw a dead bull in a small pond a couple of drainages to the north.

Thinking that the antlers might be a good souvenir of the hunt, even if we did shoot nice bulls, I inquired if we could recover them.

As it turned out, the guides wanted to pull the dead elk from the water, so we were all on the same page.

Early the next morning we saddled up and headed out for scouting, taking along a meat saw.

He wasn't far from the bank, lying on his left side with a little over half of his right antler sticking out of the water – just enough to get a rope on.

One of the guides had done some rodeo work, when he was younger, and was pretty good with a lasso; so getting a rope over the exposed antler wasn't a problem. However, pulling a mature elk out of the water was more than a one-mule job, so the other guide joined in and both mules pulled hard on the elk, getting it to the waters edge, but no farther.

You can imagine the excitement as we got both antlers out of the water and saw just how big this bull was. These antlers wouldn't be just a souvenir, they belonged on a wall.

I didn't shoot an elk on that trip; but one of the guys got a five by five that he had skull mounted, and gave me his cape. The taxidermist put the antlers and cape together to make the beautiful mount that has hung on the wall above the fireplace at Midway Farms ever since.

We measured the bull at 353 7/8", some months later. To this date, I haven't shot one that big.

So, that's the story of the big elk that I didn't shoot.

P.S. We found no evidence of what killed the bull; perhaps it was an archery hunter or maybe a fight with another bull.

Gila National Forest | New Mexico | November 1993

The souvenir – 353 7/8"

George Wieberg and I prepare to hang the elk on the fireplace at Midway Farms, between the two whitetail deer.

One mule barely budged him, so they hooked up the second.

This is as far as they could pull him. Dick Leeper, one of my hunting buddies, is standing on the bank. That's the cape from his elk on the mount above.

The COWBOY HUNT
at the Nail Ranch

It was like a page from a western novel, if you leave out the part about how we traveled to Texas. Our camp was six ranch-road miles from the bunkhouse, in a pasture called Northeast Collins, on the historic Nail Ranch in Shackelford County, Texas. This was buffalo and Comanche country 150 years ago, but today it's half grown up in mesquite trees and prickly pear – great whitetail country, which is why we were there.

The centerpiece of camp was an honest to goodness chuck wagon — provided and tended by Mr. Bill Cauble – as authentic as the chuck wagon itself. Bill prepared three memorable meals each day, far beyond the expectations of cowboys, when chuck wagons were part of their way of life.

We wore western boots and hats, Carhartt jackets and leather gloves. Every morning we saddled up our horses, slid our Winchester 94 Saddle Ring Carbines into their scabbards and rode out in pursuit of big bucks. Rattling was the hunting strategy, so we simply rode from one good rattling canyon or flat to the next, spending a few minutes to see what would come in. It was always easy to bring in the young bucks, but the older, wiser ones were – older and wiser. Sometimes, we would tie up the horses and make a big loop, rattling several times along the way. On occasion, a coyote would come to the rattle, much to his surprise and anguish. Morning and evening we enjoyed a campfire, where stories were told and knowledge was shared. Dark comes early in November, and the campfire was a welcome respite from the cool night

We were a patriotic bunch, flying the American and Texas flags over our camp.

air. Shackelford is a dry county, so medicinal spirits had to be brought in from the outside, but there wasn't too much doctoring required.

Whitetail hunting is an early morning and late afternoon activity, so there was time during the mid-day for some loafing and napping. Typically I would bring a swinging metal target and a couple of old .22 rifles – perhaps a Winchester Model 1890 pump action or a 1902 bolt action – always something different. One year I brought a Winchester Thumb Trigger Model .22 single shot; and that was a surprise and treat for everyone.

The original Cowboy Hunts, at the Nail Ranch, are gone now; but they remain some of the most memorable and enjoyable hunting experiences of my life.

Western Camp | The Nail Ranch | Albany, Texas | November 2008

Bill Cauble is the real deal; his chuck wagon meals and storytelling are legendary. My rifle is a Winchester Model 1894 SRC in 30-30.

We didn't always shoot nice bucks like this, but we did have a great time – and solved many problems of the world.

Bullet casting, using the campfire to melt the lead.

There are a lot of coyotes at the Nail and sometimes they are close enough and hold still long enough to regret it.

Jack Ogilvie, a professional salesman in his real job, takes the week off to serve as one of our guides. Here he is rattling up a buck.

153

BUFFALO on the GREAT PLAINS

This is an old bull, with a prime hide. Yes, it was really cold!

A 650 grain lead slug, one half inch in diameter, moving across the prairie at about 1250 feet per second; what in the world would something like that be good for? Buffalo! At least that was the thought in 1872, the year Sharps introduced the 50/90 Sharps cartridge, and again in 2005 – on this buffalo hunt.

The 50/90, often called the 'Big 50', was the biggest and baddest of the buffalo cartridges, which for me at least was a good reason to want a rifle so chambered. And let's not forget that Billy Dixon used the 50-90 Sharps for his miraculous shot at Adobe Walls, Texas in 1874.

Growing up in the fifties and sixties, there were still a few buffalo nickels in circulation, and of course buffalo were often depicted in the western comics. So, I knew what a buffalo looked like; but it was 1971 at Custer State Park, South Dakota where I first saw one.

They say the heaviest, thickest hides are taken during the coldest part of winter – January and February; by March the bulls begin rubbing, in preparation for spring. We were there in early January; the weather was beautiful – clear skies and bright sunshine, but the high daytime temperature was negative 5 degrees Fahrenheit.

The hunt itself was pretty routine; we drove out on the ranch, away from headquarters, and into a rolling pasture containing 4,000 acres (a little over six square miles). During the fall roundup, they had separated the seven and eight year old bulls from the herd and moved them into this pasture. These were the most-desirable trophies, and no longer prime breeding stock, so the ranch wanted to cull them from the herd.

The bulls were in small groups of ten to 40 animals, and weren't afraid of the pickup – holding and facing us about 100 yards off. We drove around for a spell, looking over several small herds and finally decided on one particular bull that had massive horns, lots of dark hair on his head and rump, but with tan hair on his shoulders. I slipped out of the pickup, took a sitting position with crossed sticks and fired. The 650 grain lead slug met a ton of meat and bones. The old time buffalo hunters, of the 1870's wouldn't have had it so easy.

Triple U Buffalo Ranch | Fort Pierre, South Dakota | 3 January 2005

A small herd of buffalo grazing on the open hillside.

Parts of the movie Dances with Wolves (1990) were filmed on this ranch, located a few miles northwest of Pierre, South Dakota.

The folks at Shilo Sharps, in Big Timber, Montana make fine rifles. Mine is an 1874 Long Range Express, chambered in 50-90, with several custom features.

This is Kevin Costner's shack in the movie Dances with Wolves. (L-R) Bob McNulty, Aaron Oelger, Dennis Holdmeier, Ryan Fischer, myself, Matt Fleming and David Lichtenstein.

Trying to be as traditional as possible, I am shooting from crossed sticks.

We Spent the
NIGHT in the
MOUNTAINS

Jeff Larkin (left), myself and Matt Fleming with their nice rams. We left the horses on the green flat above my head.

At 5:30 in the evening, the three rams abruptly filed down from the rim rock and began to graze on the high, rolling pasture. We had watched a band of nine rams the day before, but they were farther out and hadn't yet started to graze by 6:30; so we decided to pull out, ride back to spike camp and try again tomorrow.

The next morning we saddled up and made the three hour trip back, tied up the horses and eased into position below the top of a ridge; but the sheep were not where we had left them. Glassing around we found a group of three – including two big ones — comfortably bedded in the rocks a bit closer than those of yesterday. It was 11:00 a.m. and now it became a waiting game — from a mile away.

A large drainage separated us from the sheep and once they started to move, it took us two and a half hours to climb down to the creek, cross it twice and climb back up the other side to the area where the sheep were grazing. Going down wasn't so bad, but climbing back up was really tough.

At 8:30 p.m. the shooting started and ended with two very big, old rams on the ground. As difficult as it is to get in position to actually shoot a sheep, it's often said that the real work begins after the sheep is down. In my experience with sheep hunting, that's always been true!

Our guides dragged the two sheep together for pictures, then caped, quartered and cut them up. Their backpacks were full of meat, with the heads and capes tied on top. At 11:30 p.m. we started down off the mountain to the creek below; as we were above timberline and it wasn't quite dark enough for a flashlight, the going was relatively easy; it only took us an hour.

We made camp beside the creek; built a fire and cooked fresh sheep meat for a late dinner. It started to rain about 2:30 and we spent a few agonizing hours laying on the ground in our full raingear. At first light we side-hilled an hour or so to the horses; then rode back to spike camp, and the comfort of a tent – we had been away for 30 hours.

150 Miles west of Norman Wells | Near the Canol Road | Mackenzie Mountains
Northwest Territories, Canada | 7 August 2012

It had been nearly twelve hours since we had eaten our sandwiches, but now we had fresh sheep meat.

A pretty good way to end a great day of hunting – fresh sheep meat.

This is some of the terrain that Matt, Jeff and I had to navigate on the way to the sheep.

If you have never been hunting in the bush, you may not recognize this as a "superior" bush bathroom.

GOATS for TWO

A hunt is even more memorable when Brenda and I both shoot trophies – at the same time. Our guns are Rifles, Inc. Mountain Rifles in 300 Win Mag. Yes, Brenda's goat is bigger than mine!

It was Brenda, who wanted to shoot a goat; so when we landed in spike camp the guide immediately said "Brenda, I have found your goat!" The spotting scope was set up, and about two miles up the valley on the right was a tiny white speck on the side of the mountain. It was clearly a goat – a Rocky Mountain Goat! We were on a combination moose and sheep or goat hunt, so this was a great start.

Next morning we headed up the valley, enjoying a pleasant walk on flat ground, with small glacier streams on either side. Upon arriving at the drainage of the goat, it was nice to see that there were now three goats.

We plodded up through the willows to the base of the mountain, side-hilled across the rock face and on up to a ridge. It was a tough climb – everything was wet and slick. Mountain goats aren't dangerous animals, but it can certainly be dangerous to hunt them.

Everything looks different as you gain elevation. At our final position, we now saw four goats, two of which were shooters. They were bedded on a point about 350 yards out and slightly above; with nothing between them and us but open space. This was as good as it was going to get! We carefully pushed our backpacks to the top of the ridge and got into shooting position – about 15 yards apart. (muzzle brakes!!!)

The guides then jumped up and started running around like crazy, waiving their jackets and making lots of noise, trying to get the goats to stand; but they wouldn't. I left my position and eased down the hill to suggest that Brenda could shoot the big one right where he lay and when the others got up, then I would shoot. The guide turned and asked: "Brenda, do you think that you can shoot him where he is?" She had her ear plugs in and all she heard was "shoot" – which she immediately did and her goat never got up. The other goats stood and began walking away – and here I was 15 yards from my rifle.

Quickly I got back into position, just as they were going out of sight. It was a quartering shot; the Nosler 165 grain AccuBond entered behind his rib cage, and we had Goats for Two.

Wrangell Mountains of Alaska | Just south of Castle Peak | 8 September 2006

In Alaska, the Supercub is often used to get hunters in and out of spike camp.

Brenda and I take a break as we hike up the valley from base camp. That's glacier water just below us.

Our cook, in front of the cabin, at base camp.

This picture was taken at 1:00 p.m., as we started the climb. The trophy picture was taken at 5:00 – four hours later. It was a tough, dangerous climb, both up and down.

A PRETTY SHORT
Bear Hunt

The cabin; note the ropes to hold it down and the bars on the window to keep the bears out.

If you don't count the travel time from Missouri to Anchorage, then out to Port Moller on the Alaska peninsula, then the one day weather delay, then the flight to spike camp – well, if you don't count all of that time, it was a pretty short bear hunt.

Spike camp was a small metal cabin, anchored to the ground with giant ropes; evidence of how hard the wind blows there at times. There was enough space for a hunter and guide to be comfortable; but we were two hunters and two guides. After Brenda and I crawled into the wall bunks at night, our guides made their beds on the floor beneath us.

We flew in late one afternoon, as the wind let up just enough to allow our small plane to land on the beach. It blew hard and gusted all night long. When morning came it was obvious that the best place to be was right where we were, in our cozy little cabin.

About 10:30 I needed some relief from the coffee. The front door of the cabin faced the lake about 50 yards out and the standard safety rule was to look both ways for bear when you opened the door; which I did, then proceeded outside.

As I returned to the cabin, Brenda was waiting with the door open, motioning for me to hurry. From her bunk, she had looked out the small window on the south side of the cabin and saw a bear coming down the beach. You could say that her sighting was the very moment the bear hunt actually began.

The guides both stepped up to take a look and by this time the bear was directly in front of the cabin, wandering slowly down the beach, completely unaware of us. The head guide turned and said: "That's a nice bear, someone should shoot it!" When we hunt together, I always let Brenda shoot first, so she put on her shoes, grabbed her gun and out the door we went.

The wind was horrific and Brenda struggled in the gust to remain upright, but she made a great offhand shot to anchor the bear. It was a pretty short bear hunt!

Port Moller | On the Alaska Peninsula | 2 October 2009

The cooking area was basic, but adequate.

Brenda in recoil from the shot and the bear reacting.

Brenda and I got the mattresses and the guides slept on the floor. This cabin was designed for two people, not four.

Brenda with her large Alaska Brown Bear, that will square 9' 6".

The
BUFFALO
from Down Under

The horns are about 45" in width, though the picture makes him look bigger. The gun is a Weatherby 460.

The Northern Territories of Australia, mostly between Darwin and Alice Springs, is vast and remote – and the enormous ranches there are called "stations". This area would be on some folk's 'bucket list', because of the many national parks — and most especially Ayers Rock. But buffalo, water buffalo, was our reason for going there. These animals were brought in from Asia, as domesticated livestock, in the late 1800s; but today they are all feral, much like wild hogs in many states in the U.S.

One of my most vivid memories of this hunt is the rough roads and many dangerous gates. The rainy season runs October through April and as the water dries up the buffalo and cattle tracks harden, making your teeth rattle when driving around in a Land Cruiser. And the wire gates – these were strung so tightly that one person almost couldn't get the wire off the post by himself; and when you did – look out. Then, you had to close the same 'tightly-strung' gate. It was a great sense of relief each evening, when we went through the last gate and drove onto a smooth road.

The hunting was 'spot and stalk', in the pastures the buffalo shared with the cattle. Early and late they were feeding in the open areas and during the mid-day they stayed generally out of site in the brush. The grass was short on the higher ground, but taller in the low areas that held water longer after the rainy season. My buffalo was in the tall grass.

It was the last thirty minutes of light and the guide and I slid quietly through the grass, making our way to a lone bull, feeding and completely unaware of our approach. Sixty yards seemed like a fair distance for an off-hand shot; the grass covered his lower half, so I held slightly into it and touched off the 460. He showed no evidence of being hit, but ran over a slight rise and out of sight – now what?

I thought we should have waited for the truck to make the approach, but the guide insisted we walk right in. Wow, close to dark, tall grass and a wounded buffalo? We walked in slowly, guns at the ready; there he was, dead, the hunt was over. It was certainly an interesting hunting experience from 'down under'.

Adelaide River Township | Northern Territories, Australia | 16 July 2005

Our friend Roger Roberts and his wife Vicky accompanied us on this trip. Roger shot this nice buffalo.

Brenda with a nice buffalo, taken with a 300 Weatherby.

The eastern brown snake is one dangerous critter – #2 in the world, by some accounts. This view is of his underside.

Back in Sydney, Brenda and I pose in front of the tourist attraction – the Sydney Opera House.

163

Brenda with her 13 year old Stone sheep. Her rifle is a Remington 700, built by Rifles Inc., in 300 Win. Mag.

DOWN off the MOUNTAIN
at Midnight

Sheep shooting can be an evening activity, especially early in the season, when the days are quite long. Brenda and I were hunting Stone sheep on the Spatsizi plateau, way up in the northwest part of British Columbia. Our spike camp was located near a creek and each morning we climbed to the top of the plateau on horseback, tied up the horses and walked the rim looking for sheep on the sides of the escarpment.

They say that sometimes the sheep can be found just off the side and you can shoot them from the top, but the rams we spotted were a thousand yards out and 500 yards below us, so we had to stalk down off the mountain to get into shooting position.

It was 8:30 in the evening when Brenda shot. Pictures, skinning, cutting and packing takes time and it was 10:30 p.m. when we started the climb out. Although the elevation was only 5-6,000 feet, the grade was two to one, and it took us an hour to reach the edge of the plateau, stopping many times to rest. Thirty more minutes of flat-ground walking got us back to the horses, using our headlamps for light. The guides argued a couple of times about the direction, but they ultimately got us there. Now, another 30 minutes to pull the pannier boxes off the horse, pack the meat and tie the horns and hide on top.

We saddled up and headed for the far end of the plateau, where we came up sixteen hours earlier – arriving there about 1:00 a.m. As I now know, a sane person would have spent the night right there; but guides aren't always sane. Down off the mountain we went.

The only light allowed was the lead guide's headlamp. I was behind Brenda, and could see the rump of her gray mare out to about 15

It's an exciting time when all the hard work and patience delivers a sheep like this.

Brenda and I used pole and line, with bacon for bait, to catch this string of fish. Esther McGhie (left) was our wrangler.

Back at base camp, ready for the trip home, Brenda and I pose on the porch of the main cabin.

Home in the wilderness, a typical mountain spike camp.

Brenda in rain gear. It was really foggy that morning when we rode out, but it cleared in the afternoon.

feet, but no farther. I worked very hard to keep her in sight, so I could know where my horse was going. Fortunately, it was only 30 harrowing minutes down to spike camp.

I have never been really scared on a hunting trip, but several times I have been mildly unnerved, and coming down off that mountain in the dark was certainly one of them.

Elk Horn Spike Camp | Spatsizi Plateau | British Columbia, Canada | 30 August 2011

WHITETAIL with a WINCHESTER 1873

It had to happen sooner or later – 'the gun that won the west' going with me on the Nail Ranch hunt in Texas. Finding a good Winchester Model 1873 saddle ring carbine (SRC) in 44-40 was the problem; it had to be all original – not refinished or tinkered with. Also, since I like to shoot all my guns, it needed to be mechanically sound and have a great bore. And one more thing, it had to fit my budget. If you've ever been on the hunt for something that was almost impossible to find, you know what I went through. But finally there it was – laying on a table at the Tulsa Gun Show; and it went home with me.

The 1873 must have accounted for untold numbers of deer and other critters from its first production in 1873 till long beyond the introduction of the much-improved Model 1894 in 30-30; which set an entirely new standard, with the higher velocity from smokeless powder. In total, Winchester made 720,000 rifles and carbines of this model, finishing up in 1919.

Now an 1873 SRC, in any caliber, is a short-range proposition; the barrel is only 20" long, the sights are crude, the stock is low, the trigger is heavy and a 44-40 only generates about 650 foot-pounds of muzzle energy. At any rate, those were the alibis I offered my guide – telling him to get me a nice buck within 50 yards.

It was the second day of the three-day hunt before there was much activity. We had set up on an open flat, with very little cover, hoping to rattle a buck out of some dense brush – just over the ridge. It was clear and sunny, with very little wind.

We had rattled for quite a spell and were about ready to move on, when this buck came in from the left side. He was in no hurry and we watched him for several seconds. There was a two-wire fence about 50 yards out and I had

A decent 10 point whitetail taken with a Winchester 1873, made in 1892.

established that as my max distance. The buck angled up to the fence, jumped over and stopped to look around – at 45 yards. I was sitting, with my back against a small bush, and had him in my sights the whole time. He stopped, I popped and down he went – a whitetail buck with an 1873 Winchester – the gun that won the west.

The Nail Ranch | Albany, Texas | 6 November 2002

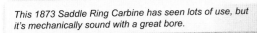

This 1873 Saddle Ring Carbine has seen lots of use, but it's mechanically sound with a great bore.

A well-equipped cowboy may have carried a Colt SAA chambered in the same caliber as his saddle ring carbine.

2002 was a pretty good year at the Nail, (L-R) Sara Potterfield, Brenda Potterfield, Larry Potterfield, John Nosler, Bob Nosler, Roger Roberts.

Bob Nosler and I are engaged in the bullet casting process. That's an original Winchester 44-40 bullet mold.

My FAVORITE FISHING Hole

Two pretty nice king salmon, 35" and 39" in length – 30 pounds or so each. Two per-person per-day is the limit.

Dad taught me to fish, back when I was just a kid; it was catfish, bass and bluegill - in the farm ponds and small creeks and rivers of northeast Missouri. Later on, older brother Marion introduced me to rainbow trout fishing in the state trout areas and I in turn introduced dad. He wasn't impressed with rainbow trout, as he could see them in the clear water but they wouldn't bite.

Growing up, we always had favorite ponds and favorite fishing holes in the creeks and rivers, all based on expectations – the number and size of the fish; but I never found a fishing hole that delivered lots of big fish – until now. And, we're not talking about three pound bass, we're talking about 30 pound king salmon.

It was on Kodiak Island in Alaska that I first heard a guide holler "Fish On". You see, when you hook into a big salmon, it's important to let everyone know, because they need to pull in their line and be prepared to move out of the way quickly – these big salmon own the river, especially when they're fresh from the ocean.

My favorite fishing hole is on the Alaska Peninsula, a couple hours by air west of Kodiak Island — in a no-name creek that flows north into the Bristol Bay area of the Bering Sea. The creeks start in the mountains and gather volume as they meander across the flat ground, on their way to the ocean.

In season the king salmon make their 'once-in-a-lifetime' spawning trip into the fresh water they were hatched in a few years earlier. For a few weeks, about the first of July, the fishing in certain places can be fantastic.

Now, there are a lot of ways to fish for salmon; typically I prefer a simple spinner, possibly with some dried salmon eggs on it, if the fish aren't biting much. It's just a matter of throwing the lure/bait across the creek, letting the current take it down stream and 'hold on for dear life'. Kings generally hit pretty lightly; but when they're on, they're on – and it takes a fair amount of time and energy to get the big ones to the bank where you can net or release them. On my very best day, I hooked 50 of these monsters – releasing all but two, so now you know why it's my favorite fishing hole.

Bear Lake Lodge | Port Moller, Alaska | 4 July 2006

Our entire group with a day's catch of sockeye salmon.

Fish or cut bait! Dried salmon eggs are a favorite addition to a spinner for king salmon – in some rivers.

A pretty nice batch of silver salmon, taken during the 2009 fall bear season – with my wife, Brenda. Silvers run a little smaller than kings.

This is about as big as king salmon get in this part of Alaska. Brenda held this 35 pounder and smiled long enough to get this picture.

The Lodge at Bear Lake. It looks pretty good after a hard day of fishing.

ONCE in a LIFETIME MOOSE

My friend, and co-worker, Matt Fleming is on the right. This is the 'once in a lifetime' moose he gave to me — and yes, he is still smiling. Notice the drop tine on the left antler. There is also one on the right.

Matt and I were on a ten day moose hunt and asked the guides to keep us together the first few days; they were fine with this and just wanted to know who would shoot first. As Matt is a few years younger and had not shot an Alaska/Yukon moose, I immediately said "Matt will be the first shooter."

The second day we spotted a big moose – a mile away; he bedded down near a cow, but the wind was bad so we decided to wait. Next morning he had only moved a couple hundred yards and the wind was better, so away we went. But, before we began the stalk, Matt said "Larry, this is a very special moose and I want you to shoot him." I looked at Matt, thought for a few seconds, and then responded "a gentleman would never turn down such a gift, thank you!" The horses took us down the mountain, across the creek and up the other side, where we tied up 500 yards downhill from the bull.

When we first saw him, he was standing at 325 yards. Cole, Matt's guide, asked if I could hit him at that distance. "Not off-hand," I replied; so he looked around and found a dead stick for support. I didn't really want to shoot from that distance and suggested we get closer; when the bull stepped behind some brush we moved up – now 264 yards – better. But he didn't offer a good shot and stepped over a ridge, so we moved up again.

The last few seconds were pretty exciting; Sam, my guide, was a step in front as he looked over the ridge; "there he is — 60 yards." I laid down my stick and stepped up to shoot off-hand. What I saw was a moose running left to right, 150 yards out – not what I expected. Retrieving the stick, the moose was now out of sight (it was the cow), but now the bull was running the same direction, and much closer. Sam gave a couple of cow calls; the bull stopped and I put a 180 grain Nosler Partition through his lungs — at 125 yards. He ran again and Matt got an off-hand shot into his ribs before he stopped. My second shot put him down. That's my once in a lifetime moose story – a gift from my friend Matt; and he went home without a moose.

Atkin Camp | Unit 15 – Yukon Stone Outfitters | Yukon Territory, Canada | 20 September 2014

This gives a perspective of just how massive moose antlers can be. Width is 64".

Matt Fleming was my hunting partner on this trip.

The cook shack doubles as the guides' sleeping quarters. Matt and I bunked in a wall tent out back.

We called this a 'Bush Monopod.' Any type of support improves your accuracy over off-hand shooting.

BULL ELK
at 10 Steps

It doesn't get much closer than this – 10 steps. That's my head in the foreground. (Photo courtesy Ken Sciacca & RMEF)

Some people say that elk hunting is like spring turkey hunting in Missouri – make a sound like a female; the male responds, comes to the call and you shoot him – simple as that. From personal experience I can confirm that this is a good strategy and sometimes it works – for turkey and also for elk.

This bull responded to our cow call from across the valley at the base of the mountain – about 1500 yards away. For 20 minutes we communicated back and forth in elk language, but he never came closer. Then all of a sudden something must have tripped his switch, as he began moving in our direction.

We got a glimpse as he came down out of the dark pines and stepped into a small clearing; he was definitely a mature bull, but at that distance we couldn't tell much. The valley floor was pasture, broken by scattered clumps of pinion trees and we could see the bull from time to time as he slowly made his way toward us. He was about 350 yards out when another switch tripped in his brain and he began to trot. But, he didn't come straight in; he was on a line that would take him about 60 yards to our right, out of sight behind a large clump of trees. What was this elk thinking?

I was crouched behind a pinion at the corner of the trees with my guide, David Allen of RMEF, and a camera crew to the rear. Then I heard him running and presumed he had caught our wind, and was outta there. But in the next instant I realized he was coming toward us – and coming fast. I went to a kneeling position, with my rifle at the ready. He came into sight at a full run and David gave a cow call. The bull stopped on a dime and turned to face us – at 10 steps. Now, what was he thinking?

I put a Nosler 165 grain Partition Gold into his chest – a bit high and through the top of his lungs. He turned and ran casually to my left as if nothing had happened; so I bolted in another round and shot him behind the shoulder at 45 yards – and it was over, except for taking pictures and this memory.

Hunting with David Allen of RMEF | UU Bar Ranch | Cimarron, New Mexico | 20 October 2011

His antlers are quite broken up, but he offered a shot I couldn't refuse.

David Allen, of RMEF, and I are watching an elk herd a mile or so away.

This Griffin & Howe Sporter in 30-06 was made from a Springfield 1903 action about 1935, but I shot the bull with modern Nosler ammunition.

David shot this nice bull a day earlier, after a long stalk through the pines.

The UNORGANIZED ELK HUNT

My first elk – and an unforgettable experience! The rifle is a Remington 700 in 7mm Rem. Mag.

It was the outfitter's first hunt; he had been a guide the prior year – and he had never hunted this ranch before. Also, he had booked far too many hunters and had to set up a second camp on another ranch - about 40 miles away. In the military they would say "Don't outrun your supply lines"; but that's exactly what had happened.

We overnighted in Montrose, expecting to head to the ranch after breakfast the next morning; however, the outfitter didn't show up till 10:30 and hadn't bought any of the supplies — so we spent the next hour at the grocery store, before heading out - (Strike 1). The ranch gate had the typical collection of locks linked together; unfortunately, our outfitter didn't have a key or combination for any of them. After an hour and a half, and several phone calls, he got it open - (Strike 2).

We arrived at camp about 4:30 in the afternoon; it consisted of a pull-type camping trailer and a couple of tents. The outfitter had to get to the other camp, so he told us to fix our own dinner and he would be back before dark.

The weather was pleasant, and two of us prepared dinner in the trailer kitchen, while the other four hunters loafed outside. They came in for dinner and sat around the table in the rear and we two cooks walked back with the pans and bowls of food. Surprise, surprise – the support legs on the back of the trailer were still in the upright and locked position. As we crossed over the axle, the trailer tipped and sat up on its behind, putting the lot of us all in one heap — with our dinner - (Strike 3).

The outfitter, also doubling as our guide, showed up three hours after dark, apologized and said he would get us up at five the next morning; however his alarm didn't go off, so we got a late start - (Strike 3+).

I only had three days to hunt, but did shoot a small 6x6 bull the last morning. That day's guide asked if I knew how to gut one, and I said yes. He said "go ahead then, as I haven't gutted one in over twenty years" - (Strike 3++). It was the most unorganized hunt you could ever imagine, and an unforgettable experience.

Black Canyon of the Gunnison National Forest | Montrose, CO | October 1990

7mm Rem. Mag. is a good elk cartridge for all moderate ranges.

We hunted in these foothills of the western side of the Rockies, near Montrose.

A typical daisy chain of locks, where each lock belongs to someone who needs access to the property.

Before the hunt - (L-R) Ross Riley from Peterson Publishing, me, J.B. Hodgdon from Hodgdon Powder and an another hunter.

LET'S GET CLOSER!

The only way you can win a fight with a grizzly bear is if you have a gun, know how to use it and can make a well-placed shot.

It all started at the beginning of the last leg of the stalk, when my guide asked how far I was comfortable shooting. My response was simply that 300 yards was about it; he said "Good, some guys claim they can shoot at 500 yards and I'm always afraid they will wound the bear."

We had been glassing all through the day in a light on-and-off mist and finally spotted this bear in the late afternoon, a mile or so away. He was eating grass at the edge of the thick brush. As we were near the bay, the most logical stalk was to back out, follow the beach for a mile or so and then proceed inland to the bear.

Our first look was a bit short, so we pulled back and hiked up the beach a quarter mile farther then turned in again. Soon we had our eyes on him, a half mile or so from the beach. This is where I got the question about how far I was comfortable shooting.

We had lots of sporadic cover and the bear was occupied with filling his stomach, so we moved pretty quickly till we got to a bush about 300 yards away. At this point, we stopped the advance. The guide didn't tell me to shoot or ask if I was comfortable taking a shot from this position, he simply stopped the stalk. Always trying to be a good client and not wanting to 'guide the guide',

I waited and glassed the bear. Finally, when I was sure that this was as far as the guide was taking me, I commented: "You know, if we back out a bit, move to the left behind cover, then come in along that line of brush, we will be within 125 yards." "Yes, but if we get that close, he will see us." "No problem, I'll shoot him!"

The guide led us forward on the line we had just discussed and soon we were there — still concealed by the brush. As the bear turned his head the other direction, I slipped out and sat on a small mound. The bear turned back and knew something was up, but I put a Nosler 165 grain Partition through his shoulders. The moral of this story is that a good guide can almost always get you closer - and closer is almost always better on dangerous game.

Bear Lake Lodge | Herendeen Bay, Alaska | 12 May 2006

Wet weather is the norm in Alaska and a wood-stocked rifle should be fully glass bedded, with a generously free-floated barrel – like this first generation Nearly-Perfect Safari Rifle.

The bear was eating grass at the edge of the thick brush. A poorly placed shot could have led to a disaster.

A truly deluxe spike camp, warm and dry. We were guests of the folks who lived there year round.

Grizzly bears vary in color from nearly-blond to nearly-black. Brenda's bear, taken on this same trip, was nearly-blond.

Fresh
MOOSE
MEAT
in the Bush

Moose country in Alaska; it doesn't get much better than this.

The Alaska moose (a.k.a. Alaska-Yukon moose) is the largest big-game animal in North America; they're also very interesting to hunt — and as a bonus, they live in some of the most remote and beautiful places you will ever see. For these reasons, and more, this was a memorable hunt.

Bull moose are huge, by any standard; if a trophy bull was standing nearby, you would have to look up to see the top of his shoulder; and a big bull moose might weigh six to eight times more than the average man. Compare that with a 150 pound whitetail or a 500 pound elk.

Getting to moose country typically requires a string of horses, an Argo, a boat, a raft or a Super Cub – and sometimes, more than one of the above might be required.

There are lots of ways to hunt moose; you can glass from the hills into the bottoms, call them in (during the rut), bump into one on the way to or from camp or float down a river and catch one in the water or meadows alongside. Moose are often in the thick willow brush and in my experience, shooting distances are short. Since moose aren't thick skinned, a well-placed bullet from a 30-30 Winchester or 300 Savage has surely worked fine – though I prefer something with a little more punch, as bears and wolves live there also.

With a big bull weighing over half a ton, even two people can't just turn him over and start gutting; as a matter of fact gutting isn't even normally part of the process. First, you take the quarters off the side that's facing up; then roll him over and remove them from the other side. Finally you get to the filets and back

Brenda and I ready to leave spike camp on a cool, but pleasant morning.

Riding and pack horses provide an invaluable service, both before and after the kill.

This is a typical Alaska-Yukon Moose. My rifle is a Rifles, Inc. custom, lightweight Remington 700 in 300 Win. Mag.

Taking a break from skinning and quartering, I cooked up some fresh moose meat — as we hadn't eaten in quite a while.

straps, the meat between the ribs and on the neck. It takes a while to process a moose; and for me at least, fresh moose meat in the bush – over an open fire – is always a special treat, if we have time for a break.

There are two lessons you will learn, or hear about, on your first moose hunt: first, no matter how challenging a hunt might be, the hard work begins when the moose is on the ground; and second, never shoot a moose that will fall in the water, because processing a moose in the water is a cold and miserable experience.

The Wrangell Mountains | St. Elias National Park, Alaska | 15 September 2006

Brenda's
MONSTER MOOSE

For a perspective, Brenda is about 70" tall. This is a pretty nice set of moose antlers.

"He's got big palms or paddles — whichever you call them —, but he's not very wide." "There are lots of points on top, but they aren't very long." "Look at his front tines, it's a shame he doesn't have good palms." These are the words a moose hunter hears and says during the long hours and days of slugging through moose country while glassing for or studying bull moose. Ultimately it's almost always a compromise, as there aren't many 'perfect' sets of moose antlers.

The first thing I look for is mass – how big are the paddles; then I look at the number and length of the points. The brow tines or fronts are of less importance and of course width is last. Some hunters only want width – it has to be a 60" moose, or bigger. For me, balance is the key; I would rather have a well-balanced set of antlers, with big paddles and lots of points, with reasonable fronts – than something that was very wide, but weak in the other areas. A 70" moose is fine, but there are a lot of 55" moose that I would rather have on my wall.

Several days earlier, Brenda and I had both shot mountain goats, spotted from base camp (Goats for Two, page 158), and had since taken a pack string several miles west to a spike camp set up just for moose hunting. The camp was on the side of a hill, overlooking a very large valley, with mountains not far to the rear. This was moose country at its very best.

Brenda shot her moose on the last day; they had spotted him from a distance, with a cow, and made an approach before starting to call. The bull would leave the cow and make an approach, then back off. The problem was that the willows were very thick. The bull sometimes got close, really close, but neither guide nor hunter could see him as he thrashed around in the willows. This went on for 45 minutes.

Finally the guide saw movement, at about 30 yards, and figured out which end was which. The shot was through the brush with a 300 Win. Mag. 180 grain Nosler Partition. The bull exploded out of the brush, ran a few yards and fell. The hunt was over!

The Wrangell Mountains | St. Elias National Park, Alaska | 19 September 2006

Brenda and 'The Monster Moose.'

Base camp. Please note the hip boots;
moose seem to like swampy areas.

The horses took us from one glassing location to the next.
The backpacks held our rain gear and lunch.

Brenda's
FIRST ELK

Brenda with her first elk. She used a Remington 700 in 30-06.

A friend from ATK/Blount said to me "Larry, if you ever want to take Brenda on a nice elk hunt, I can recommend a great place. They drive the logging roads in old Suburbans and have a wonderful lodge – and a gourmet chef." Well, who wouldn't like a place like that?

When Brenda was growing up in southeast Missouri, dads mostly didn't teach their daughters how to hunt and shoot – such activities being reserved for boys; Brenda's dad was a hunter – mostly quail and squirrel – but never took her along. She remembers having fired a shotgun once, when she was nine or ten; but that was it. Starting before we were married, Brenda and I shot doves and skeet together, but that pretty much ended when the kids came along, starting in '74.

As Russell and Sara were growing up, naturally they wanted to tag along with dad, when I went hunting – and they did. One day Brenda and I had a serious conversation about the future, discussing how the kids were going to grow up and move away; and when they came to visit at Thanksgiving and Christmas, they were going to want to go shooting or hunting with dad – while mom was home fixing dinner. Perhaps that was the conversation that kindled Brenda's interest in hunting, because she loved spending time with our kids.

The Forbes Trinchera Ranch was 300,000 acres of mostly timber in south/central Colorado; and it was partnered with the state in the Ranching for Wildlife Program. There were lots of elk and a very-long season, so we signed up for that fall, hoping it was everything my friend had described it to be.

It was an easy hunt, as hunts go; we drove around the ranch and did our spotting from a Suburban, not horseback or on foot – and spent the nights in the lodge rather than a tent. It was the fifth day before Brenda got her elk, after a long stalk through the bottoms of Trinchera Creek. She made a good shot at about 125 yards, but when the bull didn't immediately fall, she turned and asked excitedly "why didn't he fall down, didn't I hit him?" I assured her that she had indeed hit him and very well. Soon he went down and that was Brenda's first elk – her first big game animal.

Forbes Trinchera Ranch | Ft. Garland, Colorado | 4 November 1994

Snow on the mountains was part of the outstanding scenery.

Malcolm Forbes, who bought the ranch in 1969, liked art; this bronze, that I am sitting beside, is a good example.

I also shot a nice bull on this trip.

The dining room in the lodge at Forbes Trinchera.

RAINBOWS on the FIRESTEEL

Pretty nice rainbow trout – 22 inches

In the wild and remote areas of western Canada, they use the term 'fly-out' fishing; as the only way to get you to most of the best streams and lakes is to 'fly-out' from base camp – in a small plane, with floats attached to the landing gear. At the end of the day's fishing, you fly back and make plans to fish a different river 'tomorrow' — in another remote location. The daily plane rides between base camp and the fisheries become something to look forward to, as they provide a spectacular view of the scenery and wildlife.

When fishing the rivers, there are often three choices – each generally being a single destination for the day; you can fish the outlet of the lake, where the river begins, the inlet, or along the course of the river — if the pools are large and deep enough to accommodate the landing and taking off of your float plane.

The Firesteel River runs out of Tatlatui Lake and drops several hundred feet over its 15 mile journey into the Finlay River – to the northeast. Adventurous fishermen could probably navigate the entire length of the river, with a good raft or a canoe and the ability to portage the various falls and rapids, but we just waded and fished.

Years ago, fish biologists came up with the term 'fish per mile' along with survey techniques to produce accurate estimates for fishermen and fisheries managers to work with. The number they use on the Firesteel is 6,000 rainbow trout per mile – a possibly unmatched number of fish, anywhere in the world.

Son Russell and I fished this magnificent river for a couple of days – first, at the outlet of the lake, where 100 fish per person was the expected day. Then we fished the main part of the river, below and between some falls, where we caught fewer, but bigger fish. Russell is a more serious fly fisherman than myself. I took one fly rod, he took five. Mostly we used dry flies and the fish would readily take them, even if there were no apparent rises. Everything was catch and release, with barbs down, but we did enjoy fresh rainbow trout during two different shore lunches.

The Firesteel River may not be on your bucket list, but if you're a serious fly fisherman, it should be.

The Firesteel River | Tatlatui Provincial Park | British Columbia, Canada | 3 August 2014

Front end of the main cabin – breakfast and dinner.

Our camp on the Firesteel; Super Cubs are a way of life in remote areas.

We used four and five weight rods – Russell's is bamboo.

I call this 'fish art' – old horseshoes and machinery parts welded together.

Russell's Yukon Moose

Dad and son; antlers still in velvet.

A s moose hunts go, this one started routinely – get packed and sighted in, fly up to Whitehorse in the Yukon Territories, take a bush plane to a small lake in the middle of the Canadian Rockies; then hunt for a few days.

Moose hunting has always been one of my favorite hunting trips, probably because of the location more than anything else. Nothing quite compares with the solitude and beauty of the mountains in late summer. But this moose hunt was different for several reasons – first, son Russell was the primary hunter and it's a special occasion when a man gets a chance to go hunting with one of his grown-up kids; second, we were hunting from Argos, not horseback. Argos are those all-terrain vehicles made famous in the hunting industry by Jim Shockey on Outdoor Channel. Speaking of Shockey, he's the third reason this moose hunt was different; he was our head guide.

The Argos were interesting machines. We climbed 30 degree hills, running over willows ten or twelve feet high near the bottom of the drainages. One hill we named Mount Potterfield, after an adventuresome climb to the top; and we floated across lakes – using the treads on the tires for propulsion.

Shockey's private spike camp was our hunting area and we promised not to share its location with anyone. It was very remote, with lots of game. One day Russell and Jim were focused on what they called the 'pretty' moose in a group of four. He wasn't extremely wide, but had points across the top, good pans and decent fronts. They were just about to drop the hammer, when a very 'wide' moose appeared on a ridge to the north. Quickly they pulled off the 'pretty' one and went after the 'wide' one; Russell took one shot from 'the sticks' at about 75 yards. By the time the skinning and meat cutting was finished, it was midnight. We climbed into a small tent, brought along for just such occasions, and slept till daylight; then loaded up the Argo with a complete moose (less the bones) and headed back to camp.

I didn't shoot a moose on this trip, but turned down a couple that weren't quite what I was looking for. We stalked to within 60 yards of one, that was bedded, before he stood up and stared at us for a full minute; I love moose hunting.

Shockey's Personal Spike Camp | Yukon Territories, Canada | 26 August 2007

Early the next morning, after just a few hours sleep, Russell rests his eyes a bit more, before we head back to spike camp.

Jim Shockey and Russell glassing for moose. Jim is a class act and a lot of fun to share a camp with.

The antlers of this Alaska-Yukon moose measured 72" in extreme width.

Base camp, with hot showers and soft beds, is always a welcome sight after a few days in spike camp.

Horseback Hunting
in the Mountains

Moose hunting in the Yukon – 2014; (L-R) Sam Mahood (guide), myself, Matt Fleming, and Brenan Grove (guide)

Many of my most enjoyable hunting trips have been on horseback in the mountains of Alaska, British Columbia, Yukon and the Northwest Territories of Canada. On every hunt, it was a long trip to the jumping-off points at the end of civilization, followed by a ride on a small float plane or wheel plane into some remote mountain valley – and then the hunt.

Mountain quarry typically includes the Alaska-Yukon moose, Dall sheep, Stone sheep, Mountain caribou or Mountain goat. Of course there are two species of bears - black and grizzly. I shot a mainland grizzly one year, that came into our sheep camp, but have always thought of the big coastal brown bears as the ultimate grizzly bear trophy. Wolves are also around in some areas, but I have never got a shot at one.

My hunts have almost always included horses, the availability of which the hunter can take for granted, as the outfitter arranges for trucking them to the trail head, then ponying or driving them for hours - or sometimes days - to base camp. There are always one or two horses in camp that are no fun to ride; and it's not uncommon for someone to say: "What's the 'Trophy Fee' on this critter;

I'd like to shoot him/her." If you're around horses for a while in the mountains, there isn't much bad behavior you won't observe. I've seen them spook when walking by the firewood as we left camp, watched one fall in the water when crossing a creek and had one jump in the water to take a shortcut; and of course, sometimes they buck you off. Still, horses are usually the only source of transportation if you want to hunt deep in the mountains; and they add a lot of character and conversation to a hunting camp.

Mountain hunting is a great test of your physical strength, endurance, and mental character; I've had no easy hunts in the mountains and some were really humbling. In my mind the toughest hunt is probably a cold and rainy two week combination hunt, where sheep is the primary trophy, but moose, goat, caribou and bear are also on your list. Whether you tag everything or go home empty handed, you will work your tail off and come home with a deep appreciation for horseback hunting in the mountains.

Atkin Camp | Unit 15 – Yukon Stone Outfitters | Yukon, Canada | 20 September 2014

Two guides and a wrangler are taking this pack string from the Collingwood's Bug Lake base camp, in British Columbia, to a spike camp — six hours out.

12 year old Stone sheep from British Columbia - 2011

When hunting the mountains, binoculars get the most use, but there is always need for a spotting scope.

Just finishing up at the kill site; the antlers go on last. It was four hours in 'light' rain, back to camp.

The GREAT ARGENTINA
Dove Shoot

At the end of the day, they give you a hat like this – if you've earned it.

There's more to an Argentina dove shoot than pulling the trigger and seeing puffs of feathers – though that's the best part. But answer this question: "If you take every shot in range, can you run the gun?" These Benellis hold five rounds each; can you go five-for-five on doves? If so, and if you can do it consistently, you deserve some kind of medal – because it's really, really difficult.

Let me paint a picture; you may be at the edge of standing corn rows, with a harvested field to your front, or you may be under a shade tree with your back to the roost. Your field of view is 180 degrees or so, depending on whether you rotate your hips as well as your head. But you can't watch everywhere at once, and you're constantly pivoting back and forth.

The birds come from the left, the right and from straight ahead. And they come from behind, over your right shoulder, over your left shoulder and straight over the top of your head – some almost close enough to touch with the barrel of your gun and others completely out of range. One group may be cruising with a 20 mph tailwind and the next are flying into that same wind; while others are quartering in and out – the lead may be different on every shot. Oh, and one last thing, 'darting doves' is a fair nickname – WOW! They come in singles and pairs and handfuls and strings of 50 and – and they just keep coming. You might shoot a left to right crosser at 40 yards, flying into the wind; and one second later shoot another at 5 yards, flying with the wind.

So the doves are almost constantly everywhere — enough to shoot 20 boxes of shells in less than an hour, easily 2-3000 rounds per day. And, that's part of the problem your brain has to deal with — which one(s) do you shoot? One morning I counted the time between shots — one thousand one, one thousand two. Only one time, in 20 minutes or so, did I reach the count of ten — before engaging again.

Now, you've heard a nearly complete list of my alibis, let's go back to the original question: "Can you run the gun?" Personally, my answer is yes, but not every time; it just takes more discipline and patience than I possess.

Cordoba Province | Argentina | 13 March 2014

You need to wear 'tight-fitting' gloves and bring some duct tape for hot spots.

A lightweight 20 gauge Beretta or Benelli semi-auto is the preferred dove gun of Argentina.

There is hardly ever a time when you just fire one shot. Here you see an empty in the air and I am about ready to shoot another bird.

Matt Fleming and I toasting to the morning shoot, just before sitting down for lunch. We are actually under the canopy of the roost and the cattle keep the underbrush clear.

Would this scare you?

RATTLESNAKE at THREE STEPS

Prairie dog hunting in the Shirley Basin, north of Medicine Bow, Wyoming was one of my favorite past times in the 1980s and 1990s. Back then, the more remote areas had seen little or no shooting pressure and were lots of fun. During many of those years, I would make two week-long trips, one in June or July with the kids and some Midway managers and a second trip in September, with Joe Callahan, a friend from Remington.

I've always enjoyed guns, gunsmithing, reloading and shooting – and found that prairie dog hunting (shooting) provided a great opportunity to enjoy all four. During one of the fall trips with Joe, we had positioned ourselves on opposite sides of a long, narrow ridge about 50 yards apart, laying on the ground and shooting from the prone position out into the valleys below. The shots were mostly 150-250 yards.

When the shooting slowed down on my side, I headed over to the other side of the ridge to see how Joe was doing. Hadn't gone far when right in front of me was a four foot rattlesnake laying directly across my path – about three steps away. My S&W Model 28 was in the pickup, but I was carrying a Remington 700 in 222, with a 10 power scope — not an ideal rig for shooting at three steps, but shoot I did. With the cross hairs on his head, which was only half-way in focus, I pulled the trigger. There's no way to know if the bullet actually hit the snake directly, but the 50 grain bullet travelling at 3,000 fps created quite a crater in the sand and gravel of the high semi-arid prairie, and the snake's head was gone when the dust cleared.

I picked him up by the tail and walked on over to present him to Joe, who was still blasting away. Catching my movement in his peripheral vision,

Joe Callahan in the prone position, with a 40-X Remington in 222

Rattlesnakes are going to be under the shade of a rock, if the sun is strong. Behind me is a good place to look for snakes.

The tail end has the rattles, which is how rattlesnakes get their name.

he turned and smiled as I approached; but then he immediately jerked away and his eyes got really big when he saw this huge rattlesnake, still twisting around in my hand.

We had a good laugh and took some pictures, after which I made a mental note to pay more attention when walking around in prairie dog towns. Three steps is about as close as I care to get to a rattlesnake.

The Shirley Basin | Just north of Medicine Bow, Wyoming | September 1990

This one was coiled up under a rock and the only shot was right in the middle of the coil. My rifle was a Winchester Model 65 (Browning repro) in 218 Bee – Ackley Improved.

TURKEY HUNTING
in New Zealand

A couple of Merriam Turkeys, whose ancestors were imported from the United States a hundred years earlier.

First, let me say that Brenda and I didn't travel all the way to New Zealand to hunt turkeys; we were there for chamois and tahr – mountain antelope introduced to New Zealand in the early 20th century, from Europe and Asia. However, after the main events were complete, 'do you want to shoot a turkey' was one of the questions. After we said yes, the next question was 'how many do you want to shoot?' We responded with 'one each' and didn't understand until much later the nature of the question.

The following morning we drove to a ranch about 45 minutes or so out. It was all pretty routine; we crossed a creek into ranch headquarters, then turned west and headed into the ranch – cruising through the river bottom, with snow-covered hills to the south.

We hadn't gone a mile, when our guide stopped and pointed out a large flock of turkeys feeding near the top of a hill about a half mile in front of us and to the left. We drove on down the valley floor until we were out of sight of the turkeys, then parked the car and began the stalk up the back side of the hill. These hills were pretty serious; we climbed a thousand or more feet through the snow, stopping often to rest, as it was a pretty tough climb.

At the top of the hill, our guide led us quietly through the scattered brush and into position to shoot. Brenda had a 12 gauge semi-auto and I had a scoped

223 bolt action rifle (legal for turkeys in New Zealand) – both loaner guns from the outfitter. Brenda was to shoot first, and I expected to get a shot if they didn't fly far and landed within sight. Surprisingly though, our guide pointed out which turkey he wanted me to shoot.

Brenda was patient, as always, and when she shot, all the heads went up, but interestingly not a turkey flew away. I fired – two turkeys on the ground flopping – but still nothing flew. We walked out to retrieve our birds and the rest of the flock just stood around or began to move off. They simply had no fear of humans and now we knew why the guide had asked 'how many do you want to shoot?' He would never have taken us to this spot if we had just wanted to blast every turkey in sight – apparently some hunters do.

The South Island | New Zealand | 9 June 2010

Coming down off the hill, there were rabbits everywhere and our guide encouraged us to shoot them, as they are a nuisance in New Zealand.

Wallabies are considered varmints, and we were able to shoot a few of them.

Another incidental trophy was the common brushtail possum, a native of Australia. We shot these the night before.

The preferred method of hunting wallabies is from a helicopter, with a 12 gauge Benelli; not something you get to do every day.

GUNS - A FEW of MY FAVORITES

I've always loved guns, hunting with them, shooting them, cleaning and working on them, or just holding and admiring them! Perhaps it got started while sitting quietly beside Dad in the woods and watching him shoot a squirrel in the head with his Remington .22 rifle; or seeing him kill two quail with one shot on a covey rise with his old Damascus-barreled 12 gauge.

Coming of shooting age, I enjoyed cleaning those same guns and studying how they worked. During my early to mid-twenties, while in the Air Force, my hobbies were shooting, hunting, and studying guns; and there was ample opportunity to do all three.

Starting the Midway business in 1977 allowed me to be around guns on an everyday basis, and my job and hobbies became one. Major gun shows, like the one in Tulsa, provided the greatest opportunity to learn and to buy a few interesting guns to study in more detail; and during the last 50 years, I've read every gun book and magazine I could get my hands on. With all this time around guns, it seems logical that some would became favorites; and I've written about them here.

The PARKER 11 GAUGE Shotgun

This Parker has serial number 284 and was made about 1870; please note the back-action lock.

It was a very early Parker shotgun, with a three-digit serial number and in pretty nice condition - which was what got me interested in the first place. But, the clincher was the back-action locks, which feature a v-type mainspring behind the hammer, rather than in front of it. Only a small portion of the early Parkers were made with back-action locks, so obviously I needed one for the collection.

When the gun arrived, I inspected it thoroughly and gave it a good cleaning. Except for a small coil spring that was missing, but easily replaced, it was completely functional and sound enough to shoot - with black powder loads, of course. However, as we soon discovered, there was another problem; it wasn't a 12 gauge and it wasn't a 10 gauge – no, this gun featured the rare 11 gauge chambering – Parker only chambered 124 shotguns in 11 gauge, between 1869 and 1874, and now I had one and of course wouldn't be satisfied until I could shoot it.

But, there weren't any 11 gauge brass shotgun shells lying around, and I didn't expect to find any on the internet; however, one inch brass bar stock is readily available and we did have a lathe, so we just made our own shells. After casting the chambers with Cerosafe to get the dimensions, we bored out the inside, and then turned the outside diameter, which was slightly tapered —

and finally the rim. We parted it off, then turned it end-for-end, and drilled the flash hole and primer pocket. This was all relatively easy work, but it did take time, so we only made up four – just enough to shoot. As a finishing touch, we marked the heads, using a small electro-chemical etching machine.

The loading was entirely by hand, using 10 gauge wads, which was appropriate for the 11B gauge, along with three drams of black powder and 1-1/8 ounce of shot – a standard 12 gauge load. At the range, everything worked according to plan – but only for four shots, after which we had to stop and reload before we could shoot some more.

Finding an 11 gauge back-action Parker in good enough condition to shoot was a real joy for the gun collector in me, making up the ammo and shooting it was a shooter's dream. Now perhaps I need to take it turkey hunting next spring.

In the MidwayUSA Shop | Columbia, Missouri | 12 September 2012

We marked the heads of the turned brass shells just like the originals.

We only made up four cases and loaded them with black powder, using simple, period tools.

The finished loads feature an overshot wad, glued in place with waterglass.

Yes, the old Parker still shoots, and shooting it brings a smile to my face.

Here I am standing on one of the levees with a minnow pond in the background.

SNAKE SHOOTING
with a 1911

Alot of things had to line up perfectly to make this story possible — #1, Lonoke County, just east of Little Rock, Arkansas, was the home of the Remington ammunition plant. #2, Remington was producing a new 45 acp shot cartridge. #3, the engineer who led the design team for the new cartridge, was also a shooter. #4, I was visiting the ammunition plant, to see some of our orders in production. #5, Lonoke County, Arkansas was said to be the largest producer of fishing minnows in the country. #6, where there are minnows there are snakes – wow, lots of snakes. So, when asked that afternoon if I wanted to go over to the minnow farms and shoot some snakes, of course I said yes. (Note: it was legal to shoot snakes at that time.)

The area we visited was hundreds of acres in a river bottom — a maze of levees, each holding back and separating water from the other ponds. We loaded up our 1911s, cocked and locked them and began walking the levees, in search of targets of opportunity. Since this was 'high-volume' shooting, we strapped on shell bags like trap and skeet shooters use and dumped in a few handfuls of ammo. We didn't need holsters and I walked with my trigger finger in the guard and my thumb on the safety. Six hundred and fifty #12 pellets is a pretty light load and our guns needed to be well-oiled to function well, but function well they did.

It was late spring; the grass was knee high and the snake mating season was in full swing. There were snakes swimming in the water, laying quietly at the water's edge and hiding in the grass. We walked, they flushed, we shot; and shot and shot.

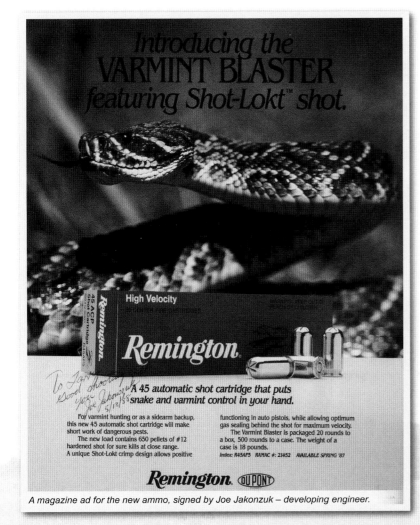

A magazine ad for the new ammo, signed by Joe Jakonzuk – developing engineer.

There were lots and lots of snakes, and it was legal to shoot them back then.

With the gun well-oiled, these 'shot loads' cycled as well as ball ammo.

My host was most comfortable walking the gravel roads on top of the levees but I preferred to walk along the narrow pathways, through the grass near the water's edge. There was more shooting activity there!

The most exciting moment was when a snake flushed from the backside of the levy, on my right, and raced for the water right over the tops of my boots. I was dancing and shooting at the same time and got him before he reached the water – on the fourth shot. Through some miracle, I never shot my boots!

The Minnow Farms | Lonoke County, Arkansas | 12 May 1988

ARMADILLO
with a THUMB TRIGGER

An interesting animal and an equally interesting gun

A couple of old .22 rifles were always on my pack list for the Nail Ranch hunt in early November. Between morning and afternoon hunts, we always had some time on our hands and shooting old .22 rifles at swinging metal targets was a favorite activity to pass the time.

One of the rifles on this trip was a Winchester Thumb Trigger Model. They only made about 75,000 of these guns between 1904 and 1923, so most people have never heard of it, much less had the opportunity to shoot one – which was one of the reasons I brought it along.

The Thumb Trigger uses the same basic sear/extractor design as all the other Winchester single shot rifles made by Winchester from 1900 to 1963, because they were all made from John Browning's original patent of 1899. But someone came up with the idea that you could shoot more accurately if you pushed the trigger, rather than pulling it.

So, the Winchester engineers eliminated the trigger and the trigger guard and simply extended the sear out the back end of the action, just below the hammer. The thumb of the trigger hand rests pretty naturally in this position; and after cocking the hammer, it's a simple matter to press the exposed tip of the sear with the thumb, to release the firing pin.

I doubt that this design is more accurate, but it is an interesting idea. One of the fun things about this rifle is to hand it to someone not familiar with the design and suggest that they shoot it a few times. Typically they don't notice that it doesn't have a trigger until they have it loaded and try to shoot it. At that time they look at you sheepishly and ask: "where's the trigger?"

One day after lunch, we had been shooting this gun and left it laying on a picnic table, while taking a break from shooting to relax in the shade. But suddenly I caught a glimpse of an Armadillo walking directly into camp about 40 yards out. Without saying a word, I got up, retrieved the Thumb Trigger and intercepted the Armadillo just as he went into a small patch of brush. One quick shot with the Thumb Trigger and the Armadillo was dispatched – possibly something that hadn't been done with a rifle like this for 75 years.

Western Camp | The Nail Ranch | Albany, Texas | November 2007

On this hunt, I also got a coyote, with my Winchester Model 94.

Around the picnic table after lunch, we blasted away with vintage .22 rifles.

The first thing you will notice is there is no trigger. But actually there is; it is just below the hammer, and you push it with your thumb.

The Nail Ranch sign, on Hwy 283 - just outside Albany, Texas, is a great backdrop for pictures.

My Favorite
PRAIRIE
DOG
Battery

My favorite handgun for prairie dogs is this S&W Model 28.

How many guns does one man need to shoot prairie dogs? Well, at least three, one for up close, one for mid-range and one for way out there. Always experimenting, I settled on a three-gun battery that made the most sense to me.

My short-range gun, out to 50 yards, was a Smith & Wesson Model 28, 357 Magnum, with a 6" barrel. Full-house 125 grain JHP hand loads were my favorite and typically I would shoot 150-200 rounds per trip. Earlier, I tried a S&W M-19 with 4" barrel, but it just wasn't heavy enough to enjoy shooting 357 Magnums through.

Mid-range was everything out of reach of the Smith 28, but not far enough out to require a scoped rifle. If the sun was shining and the wind quiet, the dogs would stand up and I could see them well enough to shoot with iron sights out to about 125 yards. For this shooting, I preferred a Remington #1-1/2 Rolling Block Sporting Rifle in 32-20 Winchester. A folding tang rear sight and Beech front, provided for the finest sight picture. I've also used a Winchester low wall and a Winchester Model 92, in the same caliber, for mid-range work; but the Rolling Block is easier and more efficient to operate, as you simply roll back the hammer, then the breech block to extract the empty case and load a fresh

round. The low wall and 92 require a second hand to operate the under lever. Whether walking & stalking, sitting at the bench or shooting off the truck door, this little rifle was always a joy to shoot and very accurate with Hornady 90 grain XTP bullets.

The third gun in my battery, and always the last one put into action, was a Remington Model 7 in 221 Fireball, with a Leupold 6-1/2 x 18 side-focus scope and a 40-X trigger. I have shot dogs with this gun out to four hundred yards on a calm day when the sun was shining; but have used it at 75 yards, shooting heads, on overcast days — with the wind blowing at gale force. I have also fired lots of 222 Remington, 223 Remington, 223 Ackley Improved and 22-250, always in Remington actions; but settled on the 221 Fireball.

This three-gun battery served me well, and on my next trip, these will be the guns I take along.

North, South, East and West of | Medicine Bow, Wyoming | June 2008

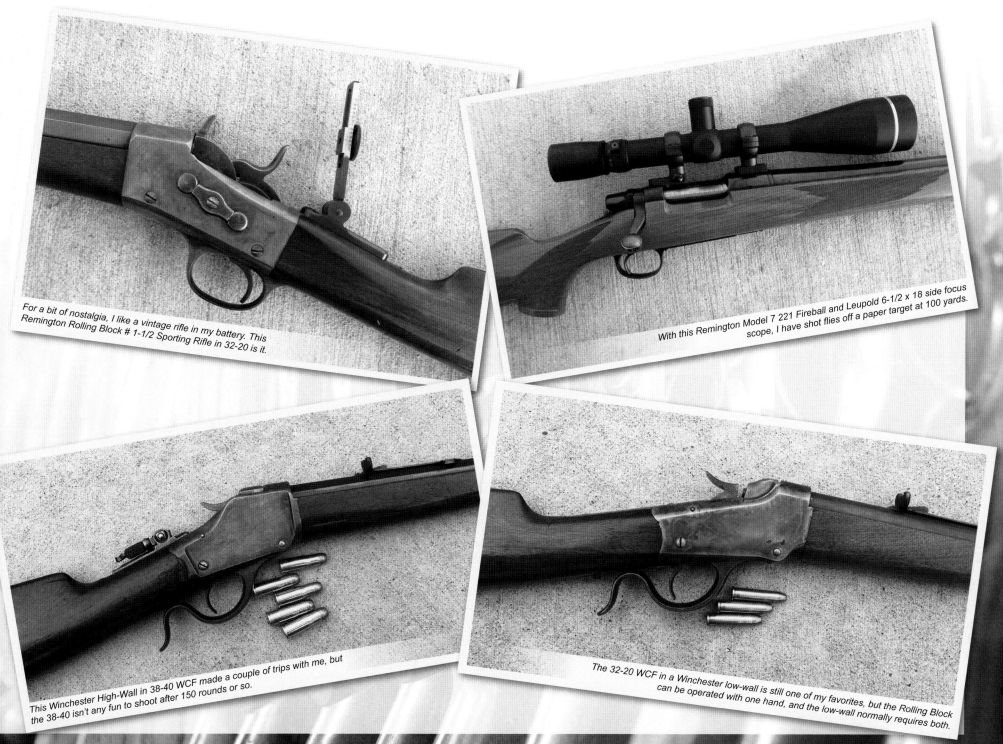

For a bit of nostalgia, I like a vintage rifle in my battery. This Remington Rolling Block # 1-1/2 Sporting Rifle in 32-20 is it.

With this Remington Model 7 221 Fireball and Leupold 6-1/2 x 18 side focus scope, I have shot flies off a paper target at 100 yards.

This Winchester High-Wall in 38-40 WCF made a couple of trips with me, but the 38-40 isn't any fun to shoot after 150 rounds or so.

The 32-20 WCF in a Winchester low-wall is still one of my favorites, but the Rolling Block can be operated with one hand, and the low-wall normally requires both.

My FAVORITE SHOTGUN
for Pheasants

There is nothing much better than a favorite gun – except perhaps having more than one!

Guns have been an important part of my life, since I was old enough to shoot – guns to hunt with, guns to shoot, and also guns for collecting. Often I'm asked which gun is my favorite; but there's no simple answer to that question. You see, being a shooter, a hunter and a collector, and having quite a few years of experience, I have many favorite guns; it just depends on what I'm hunting or shooting.

Pheasant hunting has lots of different facets — early season, late season, wild birds and released birds. While I've hunted all of these, most of my experience has been with released birds — sometimes on game farms here in Missouri, but other times on the vast prairies of the Dakotas. In my experience, released pheasants generally hold tighter for the dogs and fly a little slower than the wild ones. Wild birds typically require more lead, heavier loads and tighter chokes.

So my favorite shotgun, for most of the pheasant hunting that I get to do, is a 20 gauge over and under, choked improved cylinder and modified - that I've had for several years. Now remember I'm also a gun collector and always prefer a vintage gun to something more modern. This is a Belgian-made Browning Superposed. It's very special to me because it was made the year I was born and is documented as having been in the first shipment of 20 gauges shipped to the United States – in 1949.

On a recent hunt up in the Dakotas, I took my favorite shotgun for pheasants and also a 12 gauge side by side – in case the shots were longer. I started with the 20 and never took the 12 gauge out of the case.

Every rooster that flushed near me was down cold with one shot from the lower barrel, except for one time when we flushed a report pair. The second bird came up over my head and rather than waiting for him to level out, I tried to show off and shoot him in the head as he went over the top. I missed! Anyway, for me at least, a favorite gun is dependent on the game I'm hunting, how well the gun hits what I'm shooting at and of course it's going to be a vintage gun that could tell lots of stories, if only it could talk.

Hecla Dakota Farms, Hecla, South Dakota | 14 November 2013

On continental shoots, if serving as the backup shooter,
I often shoot my Winchester Model 12, with full choke.

My favorite pheasant shotgun is also a joy to use on doves.

Yes, of course I'm smiling – one shot, one pheasant.

Another continental shoot photo,
pretty warm weather.

207

My
BACKUP
PHEASANT
GUN

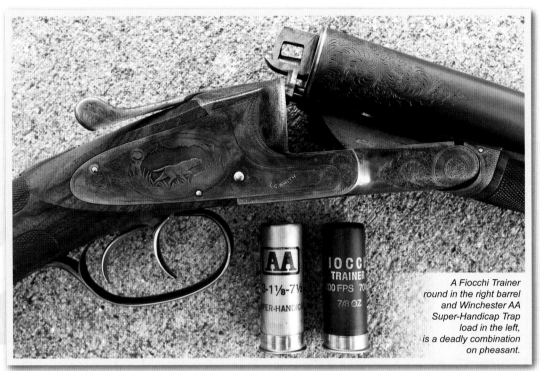

*A Fiocchi Trainer
round in the right barrel
and Winchester AA
Super-Handicap Trap
load in the left,
is a deadly combination
on pheasant.*

If the word 'backup' means lesser value or importance, then it isn't proper to call this gun a 'backup', because it's very special to me. You see, a gentleman would always take two shotguns on a pheasant hunt, just in case he has a problem or needs to loan one to a friend; and a backup gun doesn't have to come from the back row of the gun vault.

An old Browning Superposed 20 gauge, made the year I was born, is my favorite pheasant gun and it always makes the trip. My backup is an L. C. Smith 12 gauge, with double triggers, automatic ejectors and 30" barrels. During the 1990s I had it restocked, engraved and Briley choke tubes installed. Even if it was never taken to the field, it's quite pleasing to the eye — no matter how close you look.

In my mind, double triggers are the most under-rated feature of a hunting shotgun, as they allow an immediate choice of the choke and the load — because double triggers are going to mean two barrels, two chambers and two chokes. For pheasants, I like Improved Cylinder and Modified Chokes, with a 7/8 ounce load of hard #7-1/2 in the right barrel and 1-1/8 ounces of hard #7-1/2 in the left barrel. The right barrel (improved cylinder) is good out to

about 30 yards and the left barrel will go another ten. One other thing; side by side shotguns, designed for field use, almost always feature automatic safeties that slide from the fire to the safe position each time the gun is opened – pretty clever!

A lot of mental and physical activity happens quickly and often overlaps, when a bird flushes from cover. First, I acquire the bird with my eyes, re-position my body for the shot, raise the gun, push the automatic safety to the fire position, mentally decide if it will be a close shot or far, select the front trigger or the back trigger – as appropriate, swing, lead and pull the trigger. Of course, any chance at a pair of roosters typically offers one close shot and one farther out, with a quick change of the trigger finger.

At the end of the day, this old L. C. Smith, with two triggers, two chokes and two different loads, simply puts more birds in the bag than I have ever been able to do with a single trigger gun; and that's the reason it's my 'backup' gun for pheasants.

Hecla Dakota Farms, Hecla, South Dakota | 3 December 2014

A true pair of roosters and a happy hunter, with his 'backup' shotgun.

Another shotgun I often use for pheasants is this upgraded Winchester Model 21 in 12 gauge.

This L. C. Smith started life as a standard field gun in 1928, but now has an English walnut stock and forend, with fancy checkering, leather covered pad and modest engraving.

Sunday-go-to-Meeting Shotgun

With some degree of regularity, I receive invitations to participate in sporting clays events – mostly they're fundraisers, and often for the Boy Scouts or local charities. Sporting clays originated in England and came to the U.S. in the late 1980s; the first event I attended was the Charlton Heston Celebrity Shoot, put on by the NRA. Mr. Heston was there of course, as were lots of other celebrities – musicians, movie stars and politicians.

Such an event naturally requires a man's finest shotgun – his Sunday-go-to-Meeting shotgun; unfortunately, I didn't have one. But the wheels began to turn, and the gun came together in my head. It had to be a respected brand, a trouble-free design, stocked and choked so I could shoot it well, and the overall appearance had to turn heads – at least that was, and still is, my definition of a Sunday-go-to-Meeting shotgun.

The basic gun came to me in a trade at the Tulsa Gun Show the following year. It was a Browning Superposed 12 gauge, grade V (Diana), made in 1955; but it was choked and stocked for trapshooting. This was a great start; a man who owns a Browning Superposed will never have to apologize to anyone because he bought 'second best.'

The factory engraving on the Diana grade is relief carved game scenes — ducks on the right side, pheasants on the left and a pair of partridge on the bottom. Rather than bluing the receiver, Browning used a French gray finish; it naturally draws the eye to the receiver and the beautiful engraving.

The stock and forend needed replacing, first because they weren't pretty enough and second because the stock didn't fit me. English walnut is unchallenged as the finest wood for stockmaking; and exhibition grade pieces can be truly amazing. A blonde background with serious mineral streaks and feather, lightly stained, with a durable high-gloss finish was my choice; and factory-style 28 line per inch checkering panels completed the restocking job.

The last piece of the puzzle was the chokes; they were modified and full. Thin-wall choke tubes by Briley was the answer; they machined the muzzles to accommodate the tubes and furnished two skeet-choked tubes and one each in improved cylinder, modified and full. With the right chokes, I have shot everything from American skeet to live pigeon; and at those 'special events', this Sunday-go-to-Meeting shotgun has turned a lot of heads.

MidwayUSA | Columbia, Missouri | 18 November 2014

The 1993 Charlton Heston Celebrity Shoot was a classic opportunity to show off a Sunday-go-to-Meeting shotgun, but I didn't have one. That's Mr. Heston to my left.

Browning used a French gray finish, which allows the engraving to really stand out.

Sporting Clays; when the squad is ready, the first shooter steps into position and asks to see the birds.

My FAVORITE 30-30 RIFLE

For many years I've enjoyed deer hunting on the Nail Ranch, near Abilene, Texas; usually, I take my favorite 30-30.

It just seems right for a man to have a 30-30 lever action rifle and to find the time to use it, for its intended purpose. For me, that's mostly whitetail deer and coyotes, with an occasional rattlesnake and some target practice thrown in. Actually, my favorite 30-30 rifle is not technically a rifle at all; it's a Winchester Model 94 Saddle Ring Carbine with a 20" barrel.

The 1894 Winchester was John Browning's contribution to the design of the lever action rifle. He also designed the Model 1886 and 1892 lever actions, introduced by Winchester in those respective years. The 1894 was made in both rifle (longer barrel) and carbine (shorter barrel) versions, with the carbine standing the test of time. The model number was shortened from 1894 to simply 94, about 1918.

The 30-30 is an old cartridge; Winchester introduced it in 1895 in their 1894 lever action rifles and carbines. It was called the 30 WCF (Winchester Center Fire), and so marked on the barrels, until after WWII; then it was changed to 30-30. When the folks at Marlin began chambering their 1893 lever actions for this cartridge, shortly after Winchester, they called it the 30-30; and that name stuck. 30-30 means 30 caliber, 30 grains of powder. This cartridge was a game changer for hunters – a smokeless powder round that was powerful enough to kill anything on the continent; and the guns were lightweight and easy to carry.

Dad had a Marlin 30-30 carbine for hunting whitetail deer and through the years I've owned several lever action 30-30s made by Winchester, Marlin and Savage, but none of them ever gave me that special feeling. Then, at the Tulsa Gun Show one spring, I found what has become my favorite 30-30. Possibly the button magazine is the tipping point. It changes the lines of the barrel end of the gun, provides a slight reduction in weight and a minor change in the balance point.

This is a carry gun; it's so lightweight (6-1/4 pounds) and easy to carry that a sling simply isn't necessary. With a round in the chamber and the hammer on half-cock, it smoothly moves from the carry position to a well-sighted round downrange on a running coyote in a couple of seconds. It carries well, points well and shoots well; no wonder it's my favorite 30-30 rifle.

The Nail Ranch | Albany, Texas | November 5, 2006

Balance and ease of carry are two of the reasons I like this gun. Notice the button magazine, which improves the balance and reduces the weight to only six and a quarter pounds.

Interestingly, we never use camouflage at the Nail ranch. When the bucks are in the rut, it doesn't seem to matter.

Coyotes are always a bonus and they are fair game, whether standing still or running at three hundred yards.

My favorite 30-30 rifle is this Winchester 94 Saddle Ring Carbine, in 30 WCF, made in 1924. It doesn't get much better than this.

My favorite shotgun for rabbit hunting is this original, pre-war Winchester Model 42, in 410 gauge/bore.

My
Favorite
Shotgun
for Rabbit Hunting

Rabbit hunting is something I never give much thought to, until after the first of the year. For me, it's just a matter of priorities; you see, deer season and the holidays take up most of my spare time as the year winds down. Come January, there isn't much else to do outside — except cut firewood and go rabbit hunting.

From my experience, there are two ways to hunt rabbits – with beagles and without. I'm good for either one, but the hunting process varies considerably depending on which way you hunt. If there isn't any snow on the ground, then beagles are usually my preference – as they root around and push a lot of rabbits out of the thick cover that you just can't kick out on foot; but when there's good fresh snow, rabbit hunting can be great, with or without the little dogs.

Shotgun, .22 rifle or .22 handgun is always a decision to be made; which gun should I take? When I'm hunting with beagles, or if there's no snow on the ground, almost always I grab my favorite shotgun for rabbit hunting – a 410 pump. But when walking up rabbits, after a fresh snowfall, a .22 rifle or handgun just can't be beat; I try to spot rabbits sitting tight in the cover, then make a clean shot to the head.

A man doesn't have to pay quite as much attention, when hunting with beagles; mostly there's a lot of standing around waiting and watching. On

The Model 42 is lightweight, easy to carry and holds three rounds of ammo – perfect when the action is fast.

This is good rabbit habitat; it provides food and protection from predators – including me.

(L-R) Jerod Smothers, Dennis Holdmeier and I, with a few of the morning's rabbits. (Picture courtesy of Nate Hill)

this particular morning, there were four of us and one of the guys brought along three beagles – a veteran and a couple of pups. I was drinking the last of my coffee, prepared to drop the cup at the sight of a rabbit; but then my phone rang and I just had to take the call. So there I was with the cell phone in one hand, a coffee cup in the other and the shotgun in the crook of my arm — when out came two rabbits, only about twenty feet apart. I didn't get a shot!

We finished the hunt with nine rabbits that morning and were entertained the entire time by the three beagles, one or more of which was almost always baying on a track. Rabbit hunting will always have a special place in my heart, especially when I'm carrying my favorite shotgun.

The Wren Farm | Columbia, Mo | 11 January 2015

Before and after – you can see some of the project items: reshaping the stock, grip cap, forend tip, checkering, rifle pad, swivel studs and shortened barrel.

The Winchester Model 67 Project

In 2002, we developed a stock finishing kit, a reblueing kit and a stock checkering kit – using mostly Winchester Model 67 .22 rifles for the various experiments. Gunsmithing classes for a few Employees were a logical spinoff, and became known as The Model 67 Project. In total, 46 Employees customized a .22 rifle, changing the perspective of all and the lives of some.

The classes met four hours a day, one day a week, for six months or so. The first step was to shorten the forend about 3", then dowel and glue on an ebony block; after which the tip was filed perfectly round – as viewed from the front and side. Then the transition from the round tip to the more square area of the receiver was filed. Lastly, the top rails were rounded, rather than being left flat. A rifle pad was installed, the point of the comb was re-shaped and flutes were filed in. A small grip cap was installed and the grip was thinned to match; then the toe line was reshaped and the butt area tapered from the pad to the new grip area. Sanding, sealing and filling the grain all preceded 20 coats of oil finish – hand applied.

Checkering was difficult and time-consuming. Practice checkering began in the first class, so the students would be ready to checker their stock after the finish had cured. For some folks, checkering came pretty easy, but for a few it was more like a nightmare. Every student checkered their stock!

Metalwork began while waiting for stock finish to dry. Making a new rear sight elevator from a thin strip of metal, was the first step — what an interesting project! Each student stamped his or her name and the date on the bottom of the barrel. Barrels were shortened from 27" to 23", which of course required filing a new front sight dovetail and crowning the muzzle. Polishing and blueing finished up the metalwork.

There were several other steps in the project, like glass bedding the action, gold plating the trigger, nickel plating the trigger guard and guard screws, jeweling the bolt, and a few other things – all designed to help the students learn something more about gunsmithing. These $100 Winchester Model 67s easily had a thousand dollars of labor added, but not a single student would sell their finished rifle for a thousand bucks.

Gunsmithing Lab | MidwayUSA | Columbia, MO | 13 April 2011

Graduation day for the last Winchester Model 67 Gunsmithing Class,
(L-R) Ryan Fischer (instructor), Theo Miller, Will Hemeyer, Chris Cauley, Steve Cravens,
Jacob Thomason, Ben Shipp, Peter Eiberger, Ryan LeBoeuf, Larry Potterfield (instructor).

George Wieberg files the bottom of pistol grip flat.

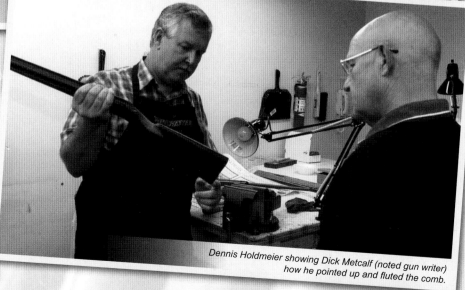

Dennis Holdmeier showing Dick Metcalf (noted gun writer)
how he pointed up and fluted the comb.

My
Favorite
Single Shot
.22 Rifle

Accuracy, out to 50-75 feet, is an absolute requirement. This rifle weighs four pounds-four ounces.

There's nothing in my childhood memories about shooting or hunting with a single shot .22 rifle. Dad had an old worn-out falling block .22, of some sort - that he used for killing hogs, when we butchered; but I don't remember ever shooting it. The .22 that dad always used for rabbits and squirrels was his Remington Model 12, pump action repeater; it was this gun with which I learned to shoot, when I was a kid.

So my experience with .22 single shot rifles, and the opportunity to choose a favorite, came after I was an adult, and began going to gun shows — building a modest collection of guns. At the larger shows, a man could observe and handle most of the .22 single shot rifles ever made. At the Tulsa Gun Show (Fall – 2001), I saw my first Winchester Model 60 and bought it. The sleek lines, weight and the balance of this little .22 were simply amazing, so I began to study it seriously.

As it turns out, this particular model was only produced for four years, in the early 1930s. The Winchester Model 60 was the sixth generation of a bolt action rifle design that John Browning sold to Winchester in 1899. From this design, Winchester produced the Model 1900, 1902, 1904, 58, 59, 60, 67 and 68, .22 single shot rifles. The 1900 had an 18" barrel and only weighed two pounds-

thirteen ounces; the Model 67 had a 27" barrel and weighed four pounds-fifteen ounces. Half-way through that run of models, Winchester achieved near-perfection, with the early production Model 60s. The early guns featured a walnut stock, without finger grooves, and a 23" barrel. During later production the stock was changed to gumwood, finger grooves were added and the barrel length increased to 27". In 1934, Winchester added a wing-type safety, made the bolt handle a little larger, went back to a walnut stock and renamed it the Model 67, which stayed in production through 1963.

The true test of a .22 rifle is whether it's accurate, convenient and comfortable to carry – looks good and works every time you pull the trigger. In my mind, there is no gun that passes all those tests better than the early production Winchester Model 60, and that's the reason it is my favorite single shot .22 rifle.

7450 Old Highway 40 West | Columbia, MO | 15 February 2015

218

The Model 67 (top) features a new 'wing' safety and a larger bolt handle. In my mind, neither was an improvement over the Model 60 (bottom).

Model 67 (top) has a 27" barrel, versus 23" on the Model 60; and the Model 60 stock is a little shorter and thinner making it more convenient and comfortable to carry.

For a kid growing up, or an adult like myself (who never grew up), rabbit hunting with a favorite .22 rifle is always a pleasant experience.

Simplicity and easy takedown are part of John Browning's original design.

Some
Things I've
Learned
About Shotguns

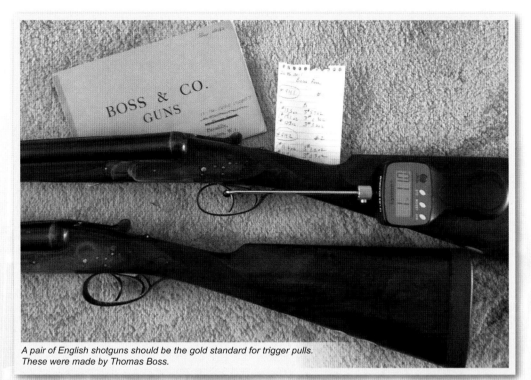

A pair of English shotguns should be the gold standard for trigger pulls. These were made by Thomas Boss.

As a shooter, a hunter and a gun collector, it's been my great fortune and pleasure to study and shoot an example of pretty much every popular shotgun made during the last 150 years – at both targets and birds. From those experiences, a few variables have stood out as seriously impacting the number of targets broken or birds bagged.

In the 1860s, English and European shotguns were re-designed to break-open at the breech and accommodate the new self-contained cartridges; Parker, Remington, L. C. Smith and Ithaca were among the first of the American makers. Side by side shotguns dominated for many years; then along came the pump action in the 1880s, the semi-automatic and then the over/under in the early 1900s. Regardless of which type of shotgun is preferred, performance is still more important than the type of action.

A good trigger pull is probably the most important, but least understood or appreciated variable in shotgun performance; and there are three parts to trigger pull – 1) the amount of pressure it takes to release the hammer, 2) the consistency of the amount of pressure required, shot after shot, and 3) the amount of trigger movement before the hammer is released. In all three

cases, less is better. For best results, the shotgun must fire immediately when the brain says 'bang'. Remember, the target or bird is moving and so are the barrels. Crisp, consistent and less than five pounds is my personal standard.

The amount of choke in the muzzle end of the barrel determines the shot pattern size and density; however, the shot size, hardness, velocity and weight of the shot charge also impact pattern size and density. A pattern that is too large and open may not connect with a target or a bird, when they meet. A pattern that is too tight and dense may pass beside the target or bird.

The last really critical variable is the fit of the stock – length of pull, drop at comb and drop at heel. If the eye isn't slightly above the rib and looking straight down the center, the shot charge will not go where you are looking.

Certainly there are other important variables, like barrel length, weight and balance; but trigger pull, choke and stock fit are the most important for breaking targets and bagging birds.

My Gunsmithing Bench | Columbia, Missouri | 24 February 2015

The choice of choke and shells (shot size, hardness, velocity and weight of shot charge) is keenly important to success.

Galazan A-10, a superb shotgun; the part we call the trigger isn't particularly important, because it simply lifts the back end of the sear, as it is pulled (see lock below).

As the back end of the sear (long piece extending to the right) is pushed up by the trigger, it pivots on the far right pin. The bent of the sear releases the back end of the hammer.

These guns are turned upside down to measure drop. Drop at heel is measured from the table to heel of butt – lots of difference.